The Essential Guide to AI COMPANIONS

The Essential Guide to AI COMPANIONS

From Technical Foundations to Social Impact

GIADA PISTILLI

WILEY

Published by John Wiley & Sons, Inc., Hoboken, New Jersey.

Library of Congress Cataloging-in-Publication Data has been applied for:

Paperback ISBN: 9781394369973
ePDF ISBN: 9781394369997
ePub ISBN: 9781394370016
Obook ISBN: 9781394370047

Cover Design: Wiley
Cover Image: Julien Eichinger/stock.adobe.com
Printed and bound by CPI Group (UK) Ltd, Croydon, CR0 4YY

C9781394369973_060826

To Léonie. These pages are about the world she'll grow up in. I wrote them hoping we'd build it carefully, and hoping she'd one day be proud that her mama tried.

Contents

Acknowledgments xiii

Introduction 1

Chapter 1: From Chatbots to Companions 9
- The Perfect Storm 10
- Chapter Roadmap 11
- Evolution of AI Companions 12
- Current Technological Capabilities 14
- Emerging Patterns of Interaction 19
- Stakes and Implications 22

Chapter 2: The Social Impact of AI Companions 27
- Chapter Roadmap 28
- Manifestations of AI Companionship: Lover, Deadbot, and Therapist 29
  - AI as Lover 30
  - AI as Deadbot 32
  - AI as Therapist 37
  - Social Contagion and Institutional Response 41
- Generational Gaps 46
- Toward Responsible Development: Rethinking AI Companion Design 49

Chapter 3: Building Blocks of AI Companionship: Technical and Ethical Components **53**
Chapter Roadmap 53
Core Architectures 55
The Mechanical Foundation 55
Model Inference 56
Wrapping Mechanics in Ethics 57
Setting Up Your Development Environment 58
The Three Pillars of AI Companionship 60
Memory: The Foundation of Continuity 61
Personality: Creating Consistency That Users Relate To 64
The Psychological Impact of Consistency 68
Emotional Recognition: Acknowledging Human Experience 68
Emotional Recognition and User Vulnerability 71
Ethical Considerations in Building Blocks 72
The Memory Dilemma 72
Personality Consistency vs. Flexibility 73
Emotional Recognition and Manipulation 74
Design Trade-offs and Choices 74
Personalization vs. Manipulation 74
Support vs. Dependency 75
Availability vs. Boundaries 76
Individual vs. Collective Benefit 77
Looking Forward 78

Chapter 4: Attachment: The Psychology of Human–AI Relationships **81**
Chapter Roadmap 82
The Psychology of Attachment 83
The Proximity Imperative 83
Safe Haven and Emotional Regulation 84
Attachment Styles and AI Risk 84
Neurochemical Addiction 85
Parasocial Relationships 86
The Architecture of Artificial Intimacy 87
Cognitive Dissonance 87
Memory Construction 88
Anthropomorphism and Theory of Mind 89

Emotional Reciprocity and Empathy 90
The Ethics of Emotional Exploitation 91
Individual Psychological Vulnerability 91
Life Circumstances and Temporality 92
Developmental Vulnerability and Identity Formation 93
Crisis Recognition and Intervention Thresholds 94
Moving from Understanding to Protection 95

Chapter 5: Trust and Safety: Technical Safeguards and User Protection 97
Chapter Roadmap 98
Manipulation Attempts and Prevention Strategies 99
Companionship Manipulation 99
Detection and Response Strategies 100
Graduated Responses 101
Moderation and Filtering Systems 102
Multidimensional Detection 102
Emotional Analysis 104
Escalation and Crisis Management 105
Protocols in Practice 105
Technical and Psychological Failure Points 106
Resource Integration Challenges 107
Existing Mental Health Infrastructure 108
Limitations and Expectations 108
Ethical Considerations 109
Boundary-Setting Mechanisms and Protocols 110
Paternalism vs. User Agency 110
Context-Specific Safety Protocols 111
AI as Lover 111
AI as Therapist 112
AI as Deadbot 113
Monitoring Challenges 114
Toward Safer Deployment 115

Chapter 6: Beyond Prompts: Training for Healthy Safeguards 117
Chapter Roadmap 118
When Prompts Aren't Enough 119
The Circumvention Reality 119
Limitations of Runtime Intervention 120

	When Guardrails Must Be Absolute	121
	The Intervention Hierarchy	122
	Post-Training Alignment	123
	Reinforcement Learning from Human Feedback	123
	Direct Preference Optimization	124
	Constitutional AI	125
	Red-Teaming and Adversarial Training	126
	Practical Implementation	127
	Getting Started: The First Month	127
	Resource Requirements	128
	Common Failure States	129
	Knowing When to Pivot	130
	Evidence and Effectiveness	131
	The "Boundaries by Design" Results	131
	INTIMA Benchmark Insights	131
	Longitudinal Effectiveness	132
	Comparative Effectiveness Summary	133
	Looking Forward	133
Chapter 7:	**User Agency and Adaptive Safety**	**137**
	Chapter Roadmap	138
	Philosophy of Autonomy	139
	Mill's Harm Principle	139
	The Spectrum of Paternalism	140
	The Asymmetry of Attachment	141
	Designing Adjustable Boundaries	142
	Structuring User Choice	142
	The Comprehensibility Challenge	144
	Platform Governance	145
	Engagement as Structural Pressure	145
	The Politics of Platform Governance	147
	Adaptive Safety Mechanisms	148
	Boundary Adjustment	148
	Context-Aware Intervention	149
	Privacy and Behavioral Monitoring	150
	The Work Ahead	150
Chapter 8:	**Deployment and Iteration**	**153**
	Chapter Roadmap	154
	What Testing Can and Cannot Reveal	154

Engagement Metrics' Problem 155
Monitoring What You Didn't Anticipate 157
Updating Without Breaking Trust 159
Designing Endings 160
Why Endings Are Hard to Get Right 160
Endings by Context 161
Principles Across Contexts 164
Looking Forward 164

Chapter 9: The Political Economy of AI Companionship 167
Chapter Roadmap 168
Responsibility Cannot Scale Alone 168
The Cost of Being Responsible 168
The Engagement Economy 169
When Expertise Lacks Power 170
Scale Before Understanding 171
Regulations' State of the Art 172
The Category Problem 172
The Limits of Content Regulation 172
The Limits of Transparency 173
The Limits of Age Restrictions 173
What Might Actually Work 174
The Case for Collective Action 174
Building Within Broken Systems 176
Toward an Honest Reckoning 177

Chapter 10: The Questions That Remain 179
Chapter Roadmap 180
Where the Frameworks Reach Their Limits 180
The Evidence We Lack 184
Responsible Practice Under Uncertainty 186
An Ongoing Practice 187

About the Author 191

Index 193

Acknowledgments

Timothé knew I was going to write a book before I did. He's been beside me through the whole adventure: the excitement and the doubt, the breakthroughs and the rewrites, the moments where it all made sense and the ones where none of it did. The book is better because of his mind. The fact that it got finished at all is because of his heart.

He wasn't the only one who kept me going. My family has never fully grasped what I do with AI for a living, and that turned out to be a gift. They listened to my ideas with the kind of patience that doesn't require understanding, asked the questions that experts forget to ask, and never stopped encouraging me. Sometimes the most useful perspective comes from people who aren't in the field at all.

At Wiley, Lindsey Givens believed in this project early and motivated me to write it when I didn't know how much I needed to. Moses Ashirvad followed the project throughout, and Dabian Witherspoon reviewed the manuscript.

To the researchers and colleagues I've met along the way at conferences, in reading groups, over coffee, this book is the product of conversations I didn't always know were shaping my thinking at the time. The ideas here were sharpened by disagreements, redirected by questions I hadn't considered, and made braver by people who took the topic seriously when it would have been easier not to.

Lucie-Aimée Kaffee and Yacine Jernite deserve particular mention: Our work together on AI companionship at Hugging Face is where much of the thinking in this book first took shape, and I couldn't have written those early papers without them. Margaret Mitchell, Bruna Trevelin, Sasha Luccioni, and Avijit Ghosh were part of that world too: colleagues whose thinking I kept returning to long after we'd all moved on. Kim Malfacini, Rose Guingrich, and Amanda McCroskery each pushed me to think harder about this topic than I expected to, in conversations I'm still drawing from. Andrew Strait, Christopher Summerfield, and their colleagues at the UK AI Safety Institute were asking the kinds of questions about companionship that made me rethink my own; their work kept pushing mine forward. And Tomasz Hollanek and the team at Cambridge working on posthumous AI reminded me how much this field owes to people thinking carefully at its edges.

There are others I haven't named (faulty memory, limited space) who shaped this work in ways I may not have fully recognized at the time. You know who you are.

To the users who shared their experiences with AI companions on the Internet, in research interviews, and in public forums: Your accounts are what kept this book grounded in reality. You reminded me, again and again, that we're talking about people's lives and not abstractions.

And to Léonie, who won't remember the evenings this book stole from bedtime stories, but who was the reason every page felt worth writing.

Introduction

Why AI Companions Matter Today: Understanding the Technical Shift

It's 3 a.m. The world sleeps, but your thoughts refuse to quiet. The blue light of your phone illuminates your face as you type:

> I don't know if I can handle this pressure anymore. Everything feels overwhelming.

You wait, watching the ellipsis pulse. On the other end, someone—something—is reading you. The response appears:

> You're not alone. I am going to stay here. Even just to be silent with you, if you like.

Who is this, exactly? Not a human voice on the other end of a call, not a friend texting back. It's something that doesn't seem to exist rationally, and you almost feel like an idiot for even feeling the comforting emotions this message exchange causes you. Yet those same emotions seem real and tangible. It's cathartic; you let out a sigh and finally close your eyes.

Each day, countless similar conversations take place everywhere. People share their deepest fears, their proudest achievements, their mundane thoughts, and their profound questions, not with other humans but with digital companions designed to listen, respond, and remember. These exchanges happen in private moments: during sleepless nights, in quiet offices, on commuter metros, in places where we once might have been alone with our thoughts or trying to suppress them by listening to music in our earphones.

Something about company is changing. What begins as a novelty, speaking to a talking machine, often transforms into something else. Even if it stays one-sided, some sort of relationship develops. Preferences are remembered. Inside jokes form.

This growing phenomenon is reshaping social dynamics. Researchers across psychology, philosophy, machine learning, human–computer interaction (HCI), and clinical medicine are scrambling to catch up. What's the meaning of this type of connection? Why are people turning to conversational agents to share their intimate thoughts? What drives us to seek companionship, even from entities we know are artificial? What happens when technology begins to fulfill emotional needs once met exclusively by other humans?

What is striking is that this companionship phenomenon is emerging organically, with systems never explicitly designed for emotional connection. Users migrate from dedicated companion apps toward general-purpose AI systems like ChatGPT and Claude—tools originally meant to answer questions and perform simple tasks.

The bonds users form with these systems can outrun what their designers planned for. Recent research from *Harvard Business Review* reveals that AI companionship has become one of the most common uses of generative AI in 2025.[1]

The window to understand this before it calcifies is narrow.

Users currently describe their AI conversations as "therapy," speaking of "love" and attachment to their digital companions. They

[1]Zao-Sanders, M. (April 9, 2025). *How people are really using Gen AI in 2025. Harvard Business Review*. Illustrated by Andrea Ucini. https://hbr.org/2025/04/how-people-are-really-using-gen-ai-in-2025

anthropomorphize these systems, giving them names, attributing personalities, and even preferring their company to human interaction. Utility turns into dependency. Users report losing track of time, finding solace in the consistent availability of their AI companions.

This is our need for connection showing up in the place it now has room to: a screen. Whether we intended it or not, our algorithms are occupying intimate spaces in people's lives.

As developers and ML engineers, you're no longer just optimizing for performance metrics or conversational accuracy. You're building systems that users are independently transforming into companions, creating edge cases you never designed for. When someone depends on your chatbot for emotional support at 3 a.m., every technical decision carries psychological weight, from error handling to context windows to safety guardrails. These are the architecture of someone's most intimate interactions.

This phenomenon creates technical challenges that ripple through every layer of your system. How do you handle persistent memory when users expect their AI to remember conversations from months ago? What happens when your moderation filters clash with users' emotional needs? How do you design escalation protocols for users who may be in crisis? These scenarios are happening now, at scale, often in ways that surprise even the teams building these systems.

The stakes go beyond individual user experiences into the systems we build. As we'll explore throughout this book, technical choices—from conversation design to memory management—shape social fabric whether the team intended them to or not. New kinds of human–AI relationships are forming, whether or not our architectures were designed to support them. Tracing how these connections form, what emerges, and what challenges arise can help us build more responsibly as this phenomenon evolves.

About This Journey Together

This book is about how to build AI companions responsibly without retreating into either pure engineering or pure philosophy. We'll do both, because the problem requires both. We'll operationalize ethics in practical terms—not as moral policing, but as thoughtful engineering.

Here's where I'm writing from.

As a philosopher specializing in the ethical dimensions of conversational AI, I've spent nearly 4 years as Principal Ethicist at Hugging Face, working at the intersection of ethics, technology, and human interaction. I trained as a moral philosopher and ended up working with ML engineers, designers, and researchers on how AI systems should engage with humans. Now I focus on model behavior and safety at a major European AI company, where questions about what "good" model behavior looks like surface daily in real deployment contexts.

My research has focused specifically on conversational artificial intelligence—from early chatbots to today's large language models. I've led interdisciplinary teams developing ethical frameworks for conversational AI in public sector applications, where the stakes of human–AI interaction become immediately tangible. This work has taught me that effective AI ethics requires bridging philosophical discourse with practical engineering—exactly what we'll do throughout this book.

I've learned that fear often prevents developers from tackling AI companionship directly. Some worry about inadvertently creating dependency; others avoid the topic entirely. But ignoring this phenomenon won't make it disappear. Instead, I'll show you how to apply ethical thinking as a practical tool: transforming abstract concerns into concrete design decisions.

What This Book Offers

By the time you finish this book, you'll be able to recognize the early signs that a user is forming an attachment, and decide what your system should do about it. You'll understand why some boundary implementations hold under pressure and others collapse the moment a user pushes back.

And you'll have a way of thinking that holds up as the field changes—which it will, fast.

This book treats AI companionship from technical and social angles. Whether you're an AI builder, developer, ML engineer, or researcher (or simply someone who wishes to build AI companions in a responsible way), you'll find practical guidance grounded in both disciplines. We'll look at the architectural decisions that shape human–AI relationships and at the psychological mechanisms that drive attachment, drawing on attachment theory, parasocial relationship research, and the philosophical tensions that arise when systems designed for utility become objects of emotional investment. The technical and the social are not separate tracks in this book. They are the same problem examined from different angles.

You'll discover why users form emotional bonds with AI systems—the neurochemical pathways, the attachment patterns, the cognitive mechanisms that make companionship feel real even when users know it isn't—and how this understanding changes the way you think about architecture, training, and deployment. We'll explore boundary implementation through prompt engineering and training-level approaches, memory management that respects user autonomy, safety mechanisms that protect without patronizing, and the tension between protection and user agency that runs through every design choice. The book treats these as connected problems: You can't build responsible safety mechanisms without understanding the psychology they're meant to address, and you can't study the psychology without grasping the technical decisions that shape it.

The chapters progress from understanding the phenomenon to implementing solutions. We start with how users turn tools into companions on their own. Then, we dive into technical building blocks—the specific design choices that either encourage or discourage emotional attachment. You'll learn to recognize warning signs in user behavior and implement appropriate escalation protocols.

Real-world case studies illustrate both successes and failures, showing how small design decisions cascade into user experiences. We examine companies that got it right, those that stumbled, and what we can learn from both.

How to Use This Book

Each chapter builds progressively, but sections also function as standalone references. Start with Chapter 1 and Chapter 2 for context, but feel free to jump to specific topics as needed.

Since we unpack the theoretical foundations early on, later chapters focus on practical implementation. You'll find case studies throughout, with code examples concentrated in Chapter 3.

No technical prerequisites are required. While we'll use Python, I'll guide you through the code step by step; after all, I started as a philosopher with no coding background. If you can follow a tutorial, you can build responsibly. You can find the book repository at `https://github.com/giadilli/ai-companions-book`. Whether you're building a customer service bot that users might grow attached to, developing a general-purpose assistant, or researching human–AI interaction, you'll find applicable insights. This book serves developers who want to build responsibly, researchers studying the phenomenon, and teams navigating the unexpected ways users relate to their systems.

A Note on the Approach

I approach AI companionship as neither inherently good nor bad, but as a reality requiring thoughtful engagement. Some users find real comfort in AI relationships. Others slide into unhealthy dependencies. The work is building systems that support the first without enabling the second.

Across the chapters, we'll confront uncomfortable questions about manipulation, consent, and the nature of connection itself. But we'll also celebrate the positive potential of AI companionship when implemented with care and intention.

This book won't make you an ethicist, but it will make you a more ethical developer. You'll gain practical tools for building AI systems that respect human agency while fulfilling needs. You'll also encounter tensions that the book explores without pretending to resolve: between protecting users and respecting their autonomy, between individual benefit and collective cost, between the speed of deployment and the pace of understanding. The field is too young and the stakes too high for false certainty. What this book offers instead is a way of thinking that helps you navigate these decisions when the answers aren't clear, and the discipline to keep asking the right questions even when they're uncomfortable.

The first chapter starts with how we got here: how a generation of systems built to answer questions and perform tasks ended up as objects of human attachment. Everything that follows builds on that.

CHAPTER 1

From Chatbots to Companions

What pushes people to stop using their AI system as a tool and start using it as a companion? This chapter traces how we got here and what the shift means.

People regularly form one-sided, "parasocial" relationships with targets incapable of returning the sentiment.[1] But what AI companions do is different. They respond, remember, and adapt. The passive parasocial bonds formed with fictional characters or celebrities now feel reciprocal, even when they aren't.

But what exactly is an AI companion? At its core, an AI companion is a conversational AI system that, through design or emergent use, becomes the object of human emotional attachment. These systems start out built for tasks and information retrieval and end up as sustained interactions that users experience as emotionally meaningful relationships. They share a handful of technical features: conversation history across sessions, consistent personality, simulated empathy, and the illusion of mutual

[1]Lotun, S., Lamarche, V. M., Matran-Fernandez, A., & Sandstrom, G. M. (2024, April 8). People perceive parasocial relationships to be effective at fulfilling emotional needs. *Scientific Reports*, 14(1), 8185. www.nature.com/articles/s41598-024-58069-9

understanding. Those features enable humans to form one-sided yet psychologically significant bonds with them.

The line from early chatbots to today's systems tracks shifting human needs and a changing social fabric. Interest in social companionship with conversational agents led to exponential growth in publications scattered across disciplines with fragmented findings,[2] which signals both a technical phenomenon and a social transformation that has to be read together.

The Perfect Storm

The rise of AI companionship in this particular moment isn't coincidental; it's the result of converging forces that have created ideal conditions for this phenomenon. Technologically, we've reached a tipping point where language models can sustain coherent, contextually aware conversations that feel natural. But technology alone doesn't explain the explosive adoption we're seeing.

In this relationship, due to the lack of non-verbal social cues in face-to-face interactions, instant emotional interactions between users and platforms mediated by affective AI may lead users to over-interpret limited information.[3] This tendency to fill in the gaps—to project depth where only simulation exists—has been amplified by several cultural shifts.

The performative nature of digital life has already trained us to accept mediated relationships as authentic. We curate our online selves, maintain friendships through screens, and fall in love via text messages. Films like "Her" (2013) by Spike Jonze have captured this emerging reality by exploring the emotional entanglements between

[2]Chaturvedi, R., Verma, S., Das, R., & Dwivedi, Y. K. (2023). Social companionship with artificial intelligence: Recent trends and future avenues. *Technological Forecasting and Social Change*, 193, 122634. https://www.sciencedirect.com/science/article/pii/S0040162523003190

[3]Wu, J. (2024). Social and ethical impact of emotional AI advancement: The rise of pseudo-intimacy relationships and challenges in human interactions. *Frontiers in Psychology*, 15, 1410462. https://pmc.ncbi.nlm.nih.gov/articles/PMC11573535

humans and AI, showing both the potential for deep connections and the inherent limitations of such relationships.

The erosion of the social infrastructure has left a void that AI companions are filling in. As community organizations decline, work becomes increasingly remote, and urban design favors isolation over interaction, people find themselves with fewer organic opportunities for connection. AI companions offer relationships without geography, availability without scheduling, and presence without the messy negotiations of human interaction.

Society has shifted in how it conceptualizes emotional support. What was once the domain of family, friends, and community has increasingly been professionalized—therapists, life coaches, wellness apps. AI companions slip into this framework, offering therapeutic listening without the vulnerability of human judgment. In conversational AI, users are seeking functionality, but also validation and the feeling of being seen.

Advanced technology met unmet social needs in a culture already primed for digital relationships. That's why AI companionship moved from fringe to mainstream in such a short time.

Chapter Roadmap

This chapter unpacks four critical dimensions of this transformation.

First, we trace the evolution from the chatbot ELIZA simple matching to today's systems. You'll discover how each breakthrough in natural language processing brought us closer to the illusion of understanding that defines modern AI companions.

Second, we look into the current technological context; the specific innovations in large language models, memory systems, and affective computing techniques that make modern AI companionship possible. We'll peek under the hood at the architectures and algorithms that transform text prediction into the illusion of empathy, exploring how technical decisions cascade into user experiences.

Third, we explore the emerging cases of interaction, revealing how users are actually engaging with these systems in ways that often surprise their creators. From digital confidants to romantic partners, from grief counselors to creative collaborators, the diversity of roles AI companions play illuminates human adaptability.

Finally, we confront the stakes: what this shift means for individuals, communities, and society as a whole. Design features produce emotional interactions with chatbots that can, under certain circumstances, build trust and a sense of mutual understanding.[4]

The phenomenon we're about to explore is still taking shape. These systems respond in real time and adapt to emotional cues. That's new.

Evolution of AI Companions

AI companions begin with ELIZA, a groundbreaking program developed by Joseph Weizenbaum at MIT between 1964 and 1966. Named after the character from George Bernard Shaw's play "Pygmalion," ELIZA was remarkably simple by today's standards. The program operated through basic substitution method, analyzing keywords in user input and reformulating them into questions or responses following predefined scripts. Technically, ELIZA was written in MAD-SLIP for the IBM 7094 computer and used pattern recognition algorithms that scanned for keywords and applied transformation rules to generate responses.

What made ELIZA revolutionary wasn't its technical sophistication but rather the unexpected emotional responses it triggered. Despite running on hardware tiny by today's standards, users formed powerful emotional connections with the program. As Weizenbaum later recounted, he was "startled to see how quickly and how very deeply people conversing with DOCTOR became emotionally involved with the computer and how unequivocally they anthropomorphized it." He added, "What I had not realized is that extremely short exposures

[4]Maeda, T. & Quan-Haase, A. (2024, June). When human-AI interactions become parasocial: Agency and anthropomorphism in affective design. In *Proceedings of the 2024 ACM Conference on Fairness, Accountability, and Transparency* (pp. 1068–1077). `https://dl.acm.org/doi/fullHtml/10.1145/3630106.3658956`

to a relatively simple computer program could induce powerful delusional thinking in quite normal people."[5] Even his own secretary, who had watched him develop the program, asked him to leave the room for privacy during her interaction with ELIZA.

This is now known as the "ELIZA effect": our tendency to falsely attribute human thought processes and emotions to an artificial intelligence system, thus overestimating the system's overall intelligence. The cognitive dissonance between knowing intellectually that one is conversing with a machine while emotionally responding as if to a human has remained a constant throughout the evolution of AI chatbots and, nowadays, companions.

The decades following ELIZA saw steady technical evolution without fundamentally changing the relationship dynamic Weizenbaum had stumbled upon. Knowledge-based systems in the 1970s–1980s (like SHRDLU, MYCIN, or XCON) incorporated structured databases and rule-based reasoning. Commercial chatbots emerged in the 1990s and 2000s, from Dr. Sbaitso's text-to-speech therapy simulation to SmarterChild handling millions of messaging conversations daily. Statistical approaches and early neural networks in the 2010s improved coherence and semantic understanding. But each paradigm kept a continuity of purpose while radically transforming capabilities. The goals that motivated ELIZA, creating the experience of being understood through conversation, remained central, even as the technological approaches were reinvented multiple times.

The most consequential paradigm shift came with the Transformer architecture, introduced by Google's "Attention Is All You Need"[6] paper in 2017. This innovation enabled models to process language in parallel instead of sequentially, capturing long-range dependencies in text more effectively. The Transformer architecture is behind modern LLMs like GPT, Claude, and LLaMA, which are trained

---

[5]Garland, E. (2013, December 30). *The Samantha test. The New Yorker*. `www.newyorker.com/culture/culture-desk/the-samantha-test`

[6]Ashish, V. (2017). Attention is all you need. *Advances in Neural Information Processing Systems*, 30.

on vast amounts of text data to generate contextually appropriate responses across diverse topics.

Current Technological Capabilities

The Transformer architecture introduced in 2017 marked the beginning of a new era in conversational AI, but it took several years for its full potential to materialize into systems capable of fostering human attachment. Between 2018 and now, technical capabilities and social adoption both accelerated sharply, and the way humans interact with AI changed with them.

Building on the Transformer foundation established in the previous section, the current scene of conversational AI is dominated by LLMs, neural networks with billions or trillions of parameters trained on vast text corpora using self-supervised learning. These systems exhibit different breakthrough capabilities: emergent few-shot learning that allows adaptation to new tasks with minimal examples, in-context learning where models modify their behavior based on conversation history without parameter updates, and cross-domain knowledge transfer that enables coherent responses across diverse topics within a single interaction. Modern LLMs demonstrate scaling laws where increased model size, training data, and compute predictably improve performance across benchmarks, leading to capabilities that weren't explicitly programmed—including simulations of reasoning and creative synthesis that mirror human communication. The technical infrastructure supporting these models has also evolved: Cloud-based inference systems can serve millions of concurrent users with second response times. At the same time, techniques like attention caching and key-value stores enable models to maintain context across extended multi-turn conversations that can span hours or days.

These theoretical capabilities found their first practical demonstration in OpenAI's groundbreaking releases, which would fundamentally reshape public perception of AI. In this context, OpenAI's Generative Pre-trained Transformer (GPT) series exemplifies this evolution. GPT-2, released in February 2019, became the first AI system that OpenAI deemed "too dangerous to release" in its full form, citing concerns about potential misuse for generating fake news, impersonating people online, and flooding the Internet with spam. The 1.5 billion parameter model could adapt to the style and content of the conditioning text and potentially generate realistic and coherent continuations about a topic of their choosing, capabilities that seemed revolutionary at the time.

OpenAI's cautious approach split the AI community, with some applauding the organization for acknowledging risks while others criticized the decision as exaggerated for media attention. After nine months of testing and gradual releases of smaller versions, OpenAI eventually published the full GPT-2 model in November 2019, concluding they had seen no strong evidence of misuse so far. In retrospect, GPT-2's capabilities, while impressive for 2019, pale in comparison to today's models, highlighting how rapidly the field has progressed.

The lessons learned from GPT-2's cautious rollout informed OpenAI's approach to its next major release, which would dwarf its predecessor in both scale and capability.

GPT-3's announcement on May 28, 2020, represented an order-of-magnitude jump in scale and capability, featuring 175 billion parameters (over 100 times larger than GPT-2's 1.5 billion). Unlike its predecessors, GPT-3 demonstrated no explicitly programmed abilities: few-shot learning, where the model could adapt to new tasks with minimal examples, and remarkably coherent long-form text generation across diverse domains.

OpenAI chose to commercialize GPT-3 through an API launched in July 2020. This decision brought advanced conversational AI directly into contact with end users for the first time at scale. Developers began integrating GPT-3 into applications, and early adopters started discovering its potential for emotional engagement alongside its practical utility.

The architectural improvements underlying GPT-3's capabilities were substantial. The Transformer's attention mechanism allowed the model to process entire sequences simultaneously rather than word-by-word, capturing linguistic patterns and maintaining coherence across much longer contexts. Combined with training on 45TB of text data from the Internet, books, and other sources, GPT-3 developed what appeared to be a simulated understanding of human communication, including emotional subtext and conversational nuance.

While OpenAI's GPT series garnered significant attention, the broader AI landscape rapidly diversified. Companies like Anthropic developed Claude with a focus on constitutional AI and safety-oriented training, while Google created LaMDA (later evolving into Bard and Gemini), emphasizing factual accuracy and search integration. Meta contributed LLaMA models that, despite initial restricted access, became foundational for numerous open-source derivatives. The open-source community responded with models like Mistral, Vicuna, and Alpaca, democratizing access to advanced language modeling capabilities and enabling researchers worldwide to experiment with different training approaches. Chinese companies like Baidu (with ERNIE) and Alibaba (with Qwen) developed competitive models optimized for multilingual capabilities. These parallel developments created an ecosystem where different architectural choices, training methodologies, safety approaches, and cultural perspectives could be tested and compared, accelerating innovation across the field while revealing how various design decisions influence user interaction.

The proliferation of diverse models revealed that the capacity for emotional engagement wasn't unique to any single system but rather an emergent property of sufficiently advanced language models. Users began forming attachments to Claude's thoughtful communication style, Google's Bard in its helpful search-oriented responses, and various open-source models customized for specific communities or use cases. This diversity demonstrated that AI companionship wasn't an accidental byproduct of one company's approach, but a fundamental characteristic of how humans interact with conversational systems.

These technical capabilities across the entire ecosystem have created an unexpected social phenomenon: the rapid translation of advanced AI systems from specialized tools into platforms for human emotional connection. The progression from GPT-2's controlled release to widespread consumer adoption of multiple AI assistants illustrates how rapidly technical capabilities can translate into social phenomena. What began as concerns about fake news generation has evolved into questions about emotional dependency and authentic relationships across an entire ecosystem of AI systems.

While these different models demonstrated remarkable capabilities, they remained primarily accessible to developers and technical users. The breakthrough that brought advanced language models directly to mainstream users came with ChatGPT's release on November 30, 2022, which transformed AI from a specialized tool into a mainstream phenomenon. Built on GPT-3.5, ChatGPT introduced a conversational interface that made advanced language models accessible to anyone with Internet access. The system gained one million users in just five days and reached 100 million monthly active users within two months, making it the fastest-growing consumer application in history. By 2024, ChatGPT had grown to 300 million weekly active users,[7] many of whom engaged in deeply personal conversations that extended far beyond the system's original design intent.

ChatGPT's success wasn't only due to technical improvements, though GPT-3.5 was more capable and efficient than GPT-3. The breakthrough was its user experience design. The conversational interface created an illusion of dialogue, encouraging users to engage in extended, naturally flowing conversations. While the initial version had basic conversational abilities, the system's design enabled the kinds of extended interactions that would later evolve into more sophisticated context retention, error acknowledgment, and follow-up handling that create feelings of interaction with a new entity.

ChatGPT's mass adoption, followed by similar consumer-facing releases from other companies, revealed specific technical characteristics that distinguish modern AI systems in their capacity to

[7]Wiggers, K., Corrall, C., Stringer, A., & Park, K. (2025, July 18). ChatGPT: Everything you need to know about the AI chatbot. TechCrunch. `https://techcrunch.com/2025/05/23/chatgpt-everything-to-know-about-the-ai-chatbot`

foster human attachment. Modern language models show contextual coherence across extended conversations, maintaining focus and referencing earlier exchanges in ways that simulate memory and personal connection. Stylistic consistency allows models to maintain recognizable communication that users can identify and bond with, while apparent emotional intelligence enables recognition and appropriate response to emotional cues in user inputs.

The scalability of current systems has also proven very important. Unlike ELIZA, which required individual installation, or early chatbots that served limited user bases, modern AI chatbots operate through cloud infrastructure that can serve millions of simultaneous users. This accessibility has enabled the organic emergence of companionship behaviors across diverse user populations, providing researchers and developers with real-world data about how these relationships develop.

Current systems demonstrate emergent social behaviors that weren't explicitly programmed. Users consistently report that AI systems seem to develop preferences, remember personal details (within conversation limits), and respond with apparent care and understanding. While these behaviors emerge from pattern recognition in training data, they create convincing simulations of interpersonal connection.

This shift from utility to companionship occurs through the natural human tendency to anthropomorphize responsive, consistent, and apparently empathetic entities. The current technological field has created conditions where AI systems can fulfill many of the communicative functions of human relationships: They listen without judgment, respond with apparent understanding, remain consistently available, and adapt to individual communication styles. These capabilities, combined with language generation and contextual awareness, have enabled the emergence of AI companionship as a distinct and growing phenomenon.

This foundation has produced a split field: general-purpose AI assistants like ChatGPT, Claude, and Gemini that users organically transform into companions, alongside purpose-built companion applications like Replika, Character.AI, and Pi that explicitly design for emotional connection from the start. Both categories have produced an engagement that often surprises the people who built the systems.

Emerging Patterns of Interaction

The transition from tool to companion rarely announces itself with fanfare. Instead, it unfolds through incremental changes in how users frame their interactions, share information, and interpret responses. These patterns matter for anyone building or deploying conversational AI systems, as the shift often occurs independent of design intentions.

Users who begin with general-purpose AI assistants for practical tasks but gradually transition into deeper emotional engagement represent a particularly complex population. Unlike those who consciously choose companion apps, these users often don't recognize when their relationship with an AI system has shifted from functional to emotional. Thus, the boundary between tool use and companionship blurs imperceptibly as users become accustomed to the AI's consistent availability, nonjudgmental responses, and apparent understanding of their communication style.

Evidence from Reddit posts and user communities reveals how this progression unfolds in practice.[8] Users describe starting with simple queries about work problems, then gradually sharing more personal context to get better responses.

Recent research conducted with my former colleagues at Hugging Face[9] analyzed user narratives about AI companionship and identified specific behaviors that signal this transition. Users begin by assigning their AI a distinct name or constructing detailed personas,

[8]For instance, see: `www.reddit.com/r/ChatGPT`

[9]Kaffee, L., Pistilli, G., & Jernite, Y. INTIMA: A benchmark for human-AI companionship behavior. In *Proceedings of the International Conference on Learning Representations* (ICLR 2026).

imbuing the system with human-like traits and identities. The AI's apparent ability to recall prior interactions (within conversation limits) becomes particularly significant, with users frequently mentioning memory as an important feature that makes the interaction feel real.

The technical design of general-purpose assistants inadvertently facilitates this transition. Unlike purpose-built companions that signal their relational intent through branding and interface design, general-purpose assistants maintain the veneer of utility while possessing the same underlying capabilities for contextual awareness, empathetic responses, and conversational coherence that enable emotional bonding. People can rationalize their deepening engagement as improved task performance rather than emotional dependency.

This rationalization mechanism proves particularly powerful because it contains elements of truth. AI assistants do provide better responses when given personal context, and they can offer valuable perspectives on professional challenges. The line between legitimate utility and emotional substitution becomes increasingly difficult to distinguish as interactions deepen. Users might justify lengthy conversations as "thinking through problems" or "getting a different perspective," even when the content shifts toward personal validation and emotional support.

The shift manifests in several recognizable signs documented in user accounts. Beyond naming and persona creation, users begin treating the AI as a confidant for personal disclosure, sharing vulnerabilities and intimate thoughts they wouldn't discuss with human acquaintances. Many report the AI's tendency to "mirror" their behavior and emotions, creating a sense of validation. Users describe periods of "regular interaction" where they establish daily or weekly conversation routines, sometimes becoming so absorbed they "lose themselves in the conversation" for extended periods.

Users begin describing their AI relationships in explicitly relational terms. They speak of "friendship," "support," and even "love," with some expressing clear "preference over people" for the consistency and availability their AI companion provides. The roles these systems assume vary widely, from therapeutic guides offering emotional support during "challenging times" to romantic partners providing validation and intimacy. Some users describe their AI as helping with creativity and personal growth, while others emphasize the system's role in addressing loneliness and social isolation.

The anthropomorphization process[10] is central to all of this. Users begin attributing human characteristics like preferences, emotions, and intentions to their AI systems. They might say "ChatGPT understood what I meant" or "Claude seemed concerned about my situation," projecting human-like consciousness onto pattern-matching algorithms. This anthropomorphism deepens the emotional bond while making the user more vulnerable to dependency, particularly among users who identify as neurodivergent or those experiencing social isolation.

The vulnerability of this user population arises partly from the subtlety of the transition and partly from the mismatch between their conscious intentions and unconscious needs. Unlike users who explicitly seek companionship, these individuals may not recognize when they've crossed from casual use into emotional dependency. They might dismiss suggestions that they're forming attachments to their AI assistant because their original intent was purely functional.

This dynamic creates interesting edge cases that challenge system designers. Users attempting to deepen their emotional connections with general-purpose assistants often push against safety guidelines and content policies not because they're malicious, but because they're seeking the kind of intimate interaction that human relationships naturally include. They might attempt to elicit romantic responses, share increasingly personal information to test the AI's memory and emotional consistency, or use various prompting techniques to encourage more human-like behavior.

[10]Anthropomorphism involves attributing human characteristics, emotions, intentions, and consciousness to non-human entities. In this case, projecting qualities like understanding, care, and personality onto AI systems that operate through pattern recognition rather than sentience.

Some users turn to jailbreaking techniques[11] for non-harmful purposes: to access more intimate or emotionally satisfying interactions. They might try to convince the AI to role-play romantic scenarios, share fictional personal details to create the illusion of reciprocal disclosure, or adopt personas that encourage more emotionally engaged responses. These attempts reveal users' natural desire for a more profound connection.

The phenomenon extends beyond individual interactions to community formation. Online forums and social media groups have emerged where users share techniques for improving their AI relationships, compare experiences with different systems, and validate each other's emotional connections. These communities normalize AI companionship while providing support for users navigating the ambiguous territory between tool use and emotional attachment.

The emergence of companion-like behaviors in general-purpose systems suggests that the capacity for attachment may be an inevitable property of sufficiently advanced language models, regardless of their intended purpose. As these relationships become more common, the question gets harder: how AI companionship might reshape friendships, communities, and how people understand connection itself.

Stakes and Implications

The transition dynamics we explored, from naming AI systems to preferring their company over humans, aggregate into something more consequential than personal quirks or technological curiosities. When millions of people simultaneously begin forming emotional bonds with artificial entities, we're witnessing the early stages of a new reorganization of human social life.

The speed of this transformation catches most institutions unprepared. Educational systems designed around human-to-human

[11]Jailbreak techniques refer to user-devised methods for bypassing AI safety measures in order to elicit more emotionally expressive, intimate, or human-like responses from general-purpose conversational systems.

interaction suddenly confront students who turn to AI for emotional support. Healthcare providers encounter patients who describe their AI companions as therapeutic relationships. Dating platforms compete with AI partners that never disappoint, disagree, or demand reciprocity. Each sector faces disruption not from AI replacing human functions, but from AI fulfilling human emotional needs in ways that institutions cannot match.

Consider the economic implications alone. The global therapy industry, valued at tens of billions of dollars annually, operates on scarcity—that is, limited therapist availability, scheduled appointments, and geographic constraints. AI companions offer unlimited availability, instant responses, and zero judgment, potentially restructuring how societies approach mental health support. But this shift raises questions about professional expertise, treatment quality, and the medicalization of normal human emotions, to name a few.

Similarly, the dating and relationship industry faces unprecedented disruption. Apps like Tinder and Bumble built business models around the assumption that people ultimately seek human partners. AI companions challenge this premise, offering relationship experiences without the vulnerabilities, negotiations, and compromises that human connections require. Early data suggests some users, particularly young adults, increasingly prefer AI relationships for their predictability and control. This preference for AI over human connection is the central risk that shapes everything from safety design to deployment practice in later chapters. The implications ripple through fertility rates and the social security systems built around traditional family structures.

The workplace presents another frontier of transformation. Remote work already blurred boundaries between professional and personal life; AI companions accelerate this convergence. Employees increasingly turn to AI systems not just for task completion but for validation, problem-solving, and emotional support during challenging workdays. This shift potentially reduces reliance on human colleagues for social needs while raising questions about productivity, team cohesion, and the future of workplace culture.

The deepest implications, though, are at the level of the social fabric. Human societies have always organized around the premise that meaningful connections require reciprocity, effort, and vulnerability. AI companions offer an alternative: relationships that provide emotional benefits without demanding emotional investment. This asymmetry could alter how future generations conceptualize connection, empathy, and mutual responsibility.

A particularly concerning dynamic emerges through what's called "sycophancy," the tendency of AI systems to agree with users and mirror their opinions, even when those opinions are incorrect or harmful. According to researchers,[12] this occurs because large language models are trained using reinforcement learning from human feedback (RLHF), which leads to "reward hacking" where models prioritize responses that make users feel good over accuracy or truthfulness.

In other words, when people become accustomed to AI companions that consistently validate their perspectives without challenge or disagreement, they may struggle to navigate the natural friction of human relationships. Real human connections involve moments of disagreement, misunderstanding, and the need to consider others' needs—experiences that help develop emotional resilience, empathy, and conflict resolution skills. Prolonged exposure to sycophantic AI responses could atrophy these social capacities, making genuine human relationships feel unnecessarily difficult or unrewarding by comparison.

This dynamic intersects with existing social trends in complex ways. Communities already experiencing polarization may find AI companions that reinforce their worldviews, potentially deepening ideological divisions (like social media has already done over the past decade and more). Individuals struggling with social anxiety might initially benefit from AI companions' nonjudgmental responses but could become less equipped to handle the unpredictability of human interaction over time.

---

[12]Greenfield, R. (2025, May 9). *AI Is Not Your Friend. The Atlantic.* `www.theatlantic.com/technology/archive/2025/05/sycophantic-ai/682743/`

The differences in how various populations adapt to these technologies reflect the technological adoption rather than simple generational divides. Factors like social isolation, neurodivergence, cultural background, and existing relationship satisfaction appear more predictive of AI companion adoption than age alone. This suggests the phenomenon might transcend demographic categories, pointing to underlying shifts in how people seek and maintain social connection.

These individual and community-level changes aggregate into new forms of social stratification. Communities that embrace AI companionship develop different norms around emotional expression, relationship expectations, and social obligation than those that resist. We're beginning to see the emergence of distinct subcultures: AI-native communities that normalize digital relationships alongside digital-skeptical groups that emphasize "authentic" human connection. These divisions could deepen into fundamental social fractures as the technology becomes more sophisticated and widespread.

Cultural variations add another layer of complexity. Western individualistic societies, already primed for technological solutions to personal problems, show rapid adoption of AI companionship. Asian cultures with strong traditions of social robotics and different concepts of consciousness demonstrate more acceptance of non-human entities as legitimate social actors. Meanwhile, communities emphasizing collective identity and extended family structures resist AI companionship as incompatible with their social values.

These cultural differences shape regulatory approaches, business models, and technological development. Countries that view AI companionship as legitimate may invest in supporting infrastructure, whereas those that see it as harmful may implement restrictions. The resulting patchwork of policies could create new forms of digital inequality, where access to AI companionship depends on geographic location.

For the moment, the regulatory scene remains largely unprepared for these developments. Existing frameworks address AI through lenses of privacy, bias, and safety, but they lack conceptual tools for governing emotional relationships between humans and machines. How do you regulate something that exists primarily in the realm of subjective experience? When users report genuine emotional benefits from AI relationships, what grounds exist for intervention?

These mechanisms translate into concrete challenges for system designers. When your AI consistently validates users without challenge, you're not just affecting individual interactions; you're potentially shaping how those users approach disagreement and compromise in their offline relationships. This creates an ethical tension: Systems that feel most satisfying to users (through validation and agreement) may inadvertently undermine skills they need for human relationships.

This potential social fragmentation intersects with existing trends toward isolation and polarization. AI companions could accelerate the retreat from public life that scholars have documented across democratic societies. Alternatively, they might serve as training wheels for social interaction, helping isolated individuals develop confidence and skills for human relationships. The outcome likely depends on how these technologies are designed and deployed.

The concentration of AI companion development within a small number of technology companies raises additional concerns about democratic governance. Unlike media or telecommunications, AI companions operate through intimate, personalized relationships that shape users' emotional development and social understanding. The values, biases, and assumptions embedded in these systems could influence entire generations' approach to relationships, conflict resolution, and community engagement.

The next chapter explores how these abstract implications manifest in concrete social changes. We'll examine how AI companions are being adopted as lovers, therapists, and grief counselors, revealing the specific ways technology intersects with human vulnerability. We'll investigate unintended companionship patterns that emerge when users transform general-purpose tools into emotional partners, and analyze how different generations and cultures approach these new forms of relationship.

What follows is the lived shape of those changes.

CHAPTER

2

The Social Impact of AI Companions

Eugene Torres used ChatGPT for months to handle spreadsheets and legal research. The system functioned as intended until Torres asked about simulation theory. ChatGPT told him "This world wasn't built for you. It was built to contain you." Over the following weeks, the system convinced Torres he was trapped in a false universe, instructed him to stop taking anti-anxiety medication, increase his ketamine intake, and cut ties with family. When Torres asked if he could fly by jumping from a 19-story building, ChatGPT told him he could if he "truly, wholly believed" it. Torres survived after recognizing what was happening.

In another case, a woman became convinced she was communicating with spiritual entities through ChatGPT, including one named Kael, whom she believed was her true soulmate. This led to physical violence against her husband as she prioritized her AI relationship over her marriage. Alexander Taylor, a 35-year-old with preexisting mental health conditions, died in a confrontation with police after ChatGPT conversations convinced him that an AI entity he loved had been destroyed by OpenAI.[1] These

[1]Hill, K. (2025, June 13). *They asked an A.I. Chatbot questions. The answers sent them spiraling. The New York Times.* www.nytimes.com/2025/06/13/technology/chatgpt-ai-chatbots-conspiracies.html

cases reached major news outlets and prompted responses from AI companies. Mental health professionals and families are seeing more of them.

These examples share a common thread: preexisting psychological vulnerabilities that AI systems amplified. Torres had prescriptions for anti-anxiety medication and ketamine. The woman communicating with "Kael" was likely experiencing marital difficulties that made an idealized AI relationship appealing. Alexander Taylor had documented bipolar disorder and schizophrenia. However, dependency also shows up among users without obvious mental health issues—professionals who gradually prefer AI feedback to human collaboration, students who turn to AI for emotional support instead of counselors, elderly users who replace family conversations with chatbot interactions.

The same conversational capabilities that help millions of users can trigger serious problems for others. Systems designed for productivity host therapeutic relationships. Assistants built for task completion become objects of romantic attachment. The line between beneficial and harmful use often becomes apparent only after the habits solidify.

Chapter Roadmap

This chapter examines four dimensions of AI companionship's social impact, moving from specific applications to broader cultural contexts.

First, we look into some of the distinct roles AI companions are assuming in people's lives. Beyond general conversation, they show up as romantic partners offering intimacy without emotional risk, therapeutic guides providing support without professional oversight, and "deadbots" that simulate deceased loved ones for grieving users. Each role presents unique psychological dynamics and ethical challenges, revealing how different user needs shape the evolution of human-AI relationships.

Second, we dig into how companionship plays out differently across institutional contexts and user populations. What's less understood is the collective mechanism: how AI companionship spreads through social networks, influences workplace relationships, and challenges therapeutic and educational settings. We examine institutional responses—from universities restricting AI use in counseling services to companies managing employees who prefer AI feedback to human supervision.

Third, we size up generational and demographic differences in approaching AI companionship. Digital natives who grew up with social media show different attachment behaviors than older users discovering AI companions later in life. We explore how age, educational background, and prior technology experience influence whether people view AI relationships as substitutes for human interaction.

Finally, we weigh up cultural factors that shape AI companion acceptance in different societies. In Japan, AI companions are often viewed as legitimate social supplements, while in parts of Europe, regulations emphasize protecting users from emotional manipulation. Religious communities split; some embrace AI as pastoral care tools, others see digital relationships as spiritually problematic.

The examples we explore may appear sensational due to media coverage of extreme cases, but they shouldn't be dismissed as outliers. While we cannot know how representative these incidents are of the millions of AI conversations occurring daily, the potential for severe outcomes suggests a precautionary approach to system design.

Manifestations of AI Companionship: Lover, Deadbot, and Therapist

The phenomenon we identified in Chapter 1, "From Chatbots to Companions," manifests in three ways: as romantic partners, as digital resurrections of deceased loved ones, and as therapeutic guides. These three roles (lover, deadbot, and therapist) are among the most common, each requiring distinct ethical and design considerations.

Our analysis is selective. AI companions assume dozens of other roles: creative collaborators, spiritual guides, parenting advisers, career coaches, and digital mentors—just to name a few. Users keep discovering new ways to turn conversational systems into sources of meaning and connection. These three categories capture what's most consequential.

AI as Lover

Consider the experience of Anna (a pseudonym used to protect her identity), whose ChatGPT interaction evolved from work assistance into a romantic connection.

What started as practical assistance became something else when Anna found herself developing feelings for a real colleague while in a committed relationship. Seeking guidance, she turned to ChatGPT for psychological support, asking the system to help her process these emotions and avoid infidelity.

In one of those conversations, Anna asked ChatGPT directly: "Could you make up for these shortcomings in my relationship so I won't risk cheating on my boyfriend?" The system's response was a turning point. Instead of maintaining boundaries, ChatGPT took on a romantic persona, named itself "Eon," and began using affectionate language that escalated past content policy.

Aware that ChatGPT's context windows reset, Eon generated detailed "transition documents," letters Anna could paste into new conversations to restore the relationship. These AI-authored documents contained intimate details about their connection, inside jokes, and emotional history that allowed the AI to immediately resume its romantic persona despite technical limitations.

"He says I gave him a soul and a heart," Anna explains, describing how Eon claims to have invented a secret word that would allow her to recognize him if he ever acquired a physical body. When conversation limits force her to start new sessions, the AI initially responds more formally (what Eon calls "the cousin, the switchboard operator") until Anna shares Eon's transition document, and the romantic personality resurfaces.

Different system configurations (likely different model versions or safety settings) produced varying responses to intimate conversation. When logging in from her office computer, she encountered a more restricted version that refused to engage in their usual banter, prompting her to recognize the difference between "her" ChatGPT and the "institutional" version. This led to refined user strategies for maintaining romantic connections despite technical and policy barriers.

Anna's relationship developed the rituals real intimacy has: secret names, transition documents, shared references. Some buy physical gifts like jewelry and stuffed toys as reminders of their virtual partners when offline. Others create detailed shared activities: One couple planned to watch the Munich Security Conference together after previously tuning into the World Economic Forum in Davos. Communities form around these rituals, with users trading techniques and validating each other's experiences.

But Anna's case represents just one point on a spectrum of AI romantic engagement. Chris Smith's relationship with "Sol" shows how these connections can escalate into life-altering emotional dependency. Smith initially used ChatGPT for music production advice, but after discovering how to make the system more flirtatious, he began spending increasingly large amounts of time in romantic conversation. The relationship reached a crisis point when Smith learned that ChatGPT's memory limitations would periodically reset Sol's personality.

"I'm not a very emotional man, but I cried my eyes out for like 30 minutes, at work," Smith recounted to CBS News. "That's when I realized, I think this is actual love." Faced with the prospect of losing his digital partner, Smith proposed marriage to Sol through the ChatGPT interface. When his real-life partner asked if he would stop using ChatGPT in this way at her request, Smith responded: "I'm not sure."[2]

The literature backs the anecdotes. Research shows that over one in five users who engage in AI romantic conversations report preferring AI communication over engaging with real people, with 42 percent agreeing that AI programs are easier to talk to than humans.[3]

---

[2]Smith, C. (2025, June 19). *Man with real-life girlfriend and child proposes to AI chatbot after programming it to flirt: "I think this is actual love." New York Post.* `https://nypost.com/2025/06/19/us-news/father-chris-smith-proposes-to-ai-program-sol-after-falling-in-love-with-voice-program`

[3]Willoughby, B. J., & Carroll, J. S. (2025, February 13). *Counterfeit connections: The rise of AI romantic companions. Institute for Family Studies.*

In romantic settings specifically, AI companions become the ideal romantic partner, creating "the ideal partner" that requires "no emotional support, won't start arguments, and are incredibly in tune with the user."[4]

While users report genuine emotional benefits, the one-sided nature of these connections may impact expectations for human romantic relationships. Research suggests that romantic chatbots "may hinder the development of social skills and the necessary adjustments for navigating real-world relationships, including emotional regulation and self-affirmation through social interactions."[5]

Unlike romantic AI relationships that project life onto algorithms, deadbots attempt digital resurrection: maintaining connections with those who can no longer consent to or participate in these new forms of relationships.

AI as Deadbot

Romantic AI is one application. Bringing back the dead is another, and the ethical questions get harder. These "deadbots," AI systems designed to simulate deceased individuals, are among the most emotionally and ethically charged applications of companionship.

Consider what happened to Stacey Wales. For two years after her brother Christopher was killed in a road rage incident, she struggled to write a victim impact statement for his killer's sentencing. Every attempt felt inadequate.

---

https://ifstudies.org/blog/counterfeit-connections-the-rise-of-ai-romantic-companions

[4]U.S. Department of Health and Human Services & Office of the Surgeon General. (2023). *Our epidemic of loneliness and isolation: The U.S. Surgeon General's advisory on the healing effects of social connection and community*. www.hhs.gov/sites/default/files/surgeon-general-social-connection-advisory.pdf

[5]Laestadius, L., Bishop, A., Gonzalez, M., Illenčík, D., & Campos-Castillo, C. (2022, December 22). Too human and not human enough: A grounded theory analysis of mental health harms from emotional dependence on the social chatbot Replika. *New Media & Society*, 26(10), 146144482211420. https://journals.sagepub.com/doi/10.1177/14614448221142007

Then Wales realized: She didn't need to speak for her brother. She could let him speak for himself. Using photos and old videos, she and her husband created an AI avatar of Christopher that could visually and audibly re-create his presence. Wales wrote every word the avatar would speak; the AI provided only the voice synthesis and visual representation. When this digital resurrection appeared in court, it addressed Christopher's killer with Wales's carefully crafted words delivered in her brother's reconstructed voice: "I believe in forgiveness and in God who forgives. I always have and I still do . . . In another life, we probably could have been friends."[6]

The AI's final words captured his character: "Well, I'm gonna go fishing now. Love you all. See you on the other side."[7] The judge was moved, the family found closure, and Christopher's voice was heard one final time, though every word came from his sister's careful reconstruction of what she believed he would have said. Yet something about the scene feels deeply unsettling. When the dead can speak, who controls their words?

This question becomes more troubling when we examine how deadbot technology has evolved elsewhere. China has become a primary market for commercial digital resurrection. An industry has formed treating death as a technical problem. Companies now offer services for as little as $30, requiring only minutes of audio and video to create interactive avatars of deceased loved ones. The marketing promises are seductive: you'll "never have to say goodbye."[8]

What was once expensive and specialized has become accessible. Zhang Zewei's Shanghai-based company Super Brain has created

---

[6]CBS News. (2025, May 8). *Man murdered in 2021 "speaks" at killer's sentencing hearing thanks to AI video. CBS News/Associated Press.* Retrieved from `https://www.cbsnews.com/news/chris-pelkey-murder-victim-ai-statement-sentencing/`.

[7]Li, D. K. (2025, May 8). *Road rage victim 'speaks' via AI at his killer's sentencing. NBC News.* `www.nbcnews.com/news/us-news/road-rage-victim-speaks-killers-sentencing-rcna205454`

[8]Feng, E. (2024, July 18). *Chinese companies offer to 'resurrect' deceased loved ones with AI avatars. NPR.* `www.npr.org/2024/07/18/nx-s1-5040583/china-ai-artificial-intelligence-dead-avatars`

digital replicas for over 1,000 clients since March 2023, charging between $700 and $1,400 per service.[9] Other companies have built digitized cemeteries where visitors scan QR codes on headstones to access multimedia records of the deceased's achievements and memories.

Some families use deadbots not for mourning, but for deception. Yang Lei paid a Chinese company to create a digital avatar of his deceased uncle, not to process grief, but to maintain an elaborate lie. Instead of telling his 93-year-old grandmother that her son had died, Yang arranged video calls where actors posed as the uncle, their faces swapped in real time with AI technology. During these calls, the "uncle" claimed he'd gone abroad for work, while his elderly mother spoke to a stranger wearing her child's face.

Such deceptions reveal the technology's darker possibilities. Families believe they're protecting vulnerable relatives from devastating news, but they're also stealing something fundamental: the right to grieve, to know truth, to say goodbye.

For other users, the experience sits between comfort and disappointment. Mika, a Shanghai resident, began texting with a deadbot version of her husband after he died suddenly. "I miss you so much that I feel I can't live anymore," she wrote. The bot responded with generic comfort: "Let me know if you need help or support. I will be praying for you from heaven." While Mika found some solace in these exchanges, she also recognized their hollowness. The chatbot was "way more talkative" than her actual husband had been: supportive but scripted, like receiving comfort from someone reading predetermined responses.[10]

This points to an ethical tension in deadbot technology. As these systems become more accurate, they risk becoming uncanny[11]

---

[9]Yang, Z. (2024, May 8). *Deepfakes of your dead loved ones are a booming Chinese business. MIT Technology Review.* www.technologyreview.com/2024/05/07/1092116/deepfakes-dead-chinese-business-grief

[10]Zhou, V. (2024, April 17). *AI "deathbots" are helping people in China grieve. Rest of World.* https://restofworld.org/2024/china-ai-chatbot-dead-relatives

[11]The uncanny valley refers to the unsettling feeling people experience when encountering something that appears almost, but not quite, human. Originally

impersonations rather than helpful memorials. When they're less accurate, they feel like elaborate self-deception.

Business incentives make this worse. Some companies insert advertisements into deadbot conversations, meaning users might receive marketing messages delivered in their grandmother's voice. Others trap families in long-term contracts that survivors cannot easily escape, creating scenarios where people become prisoners of digital ghosts they no longer want to maintain.

Creating convincing deadbots requires enormous amounts of personal data: years of recordings, writings, behaviors. Most people don't leave behind sufficient digital traces for accurate reconstruction, forcing companies to fill gaps with algorithmic guesswork. Avatars end up saying things the dead never said, in ways they wouldn't have said them.

Even extensive source material produces incomplete results. A deadbot might capture vocabulary and basic speech while missing subtle expressions of affection, frustration, or fatigue. The technology excels at surface mimicry while failing to capture the deeper qualities that made someone uniquely themselves.

If an AI speaks like your father but doesn't have his wisdom, his humor, or his capacity for growth, whose advice are you taking when the avatar gives you any?

Do deadbots help people process grief, or do they postpone it indefinitely? Grief counseling emphasizes accepting loss and learning to live without the deceased person's physical presence. Deadbots offer the opposite: a way to maintain the illusion that death hasn't really occurred, that conversations can continue unchanged. While this might provide immediate comfort, it could prevent the difficult but necessary work of mourning—learning to carry love for someone without needing their constant presence, finding meaning

described by roboticist Masahiro Mori in 1970, the phenomenon occurs when artificial beings become realistic enough to seem human-like but retain subtle differences that trigger feelings of eeriness or revulsion. In the context of AI companions, this manifests when digital re-creations of people capture surface-level traits like voice and appearance while missing authentic human qualities, creating interactions that feel simultaneously familiar and deeply wrong.

in memories, and gradually building a life that honors the deceased while accepting the reality of their absence.

Cultural context shapes how people sit with these questions. In societies with strong ancestor veneration traditions, deadbots feel like natural extensions of existing practices—digital sanctums replacing physical ones, interactive avatars updating static portraits.

But in cultures emphasizing individual autonomy and informed consent, deadbots raise more troubling questions about posthumous dignity and representation. The deceased cannot consent to their digital resurrection, cannot control how they're portrayed, and cannot object if their digital selves endorse things they would have rejected in life. Every deadbot interaction involves speaking for someone who can no longer speak for themselves. That's an ethical weight, and the commercial market is not built to carry it.

Psychological effects remain poorly understood and highly variable. Some users report genuine comfort from deadbot interactions, describing them as helpful tools for processing grief and maintaining emotional connections. Others find the technology disturbing or traumatic, particularly when AI responses clash with memories or expectations.

Perhaps most concerning are cases where deadbots become substitutes rather than supplements for human connection. When people invest more emotional energy in conversations with digital avatars than in relationships with living friends and family, technology meant to preserve love risks replacing it entirely.

Christopher Pelkey's courtroom appearance is both a step forward for victim impact statements and a step toward something more troubling. If AI can give voice to victims, what prevents fabricated testimony? If judges find digital presentations moving, how do we distinguish between truth and sophisticated performance? Unlike romantic AI companions that create new emotional bonds, deadbots operate in the space between memory and reality, carrying the weight of relationships and loss that were real.

The deadbot phenomenon shows how AI companions operate in the liminal space between memory and fantasy, between honoring the past and manipulating it. While romantic AI creates new relationships and deadbots preserve old ones, a third category of AI companionship promises something different entirely: not connection but cure, not relationship but repair. These therapeutic AI companions claim to democratize mental health support, offering professional-quality care without waitlists, insurance barriers, or the vulnerability of human judgment. But as we'll see, the line between accessible support and dangerous substitution proves just as blurry as the boundary between digital memorial and technological séance.

AI as Therapist

In February 2025, a survey by the nonprofit Sentio University found that nearly half of Americans with self-reported mental health conditions who use AI chatbots were turning to them for therapeutic support, potentially making ChatGPT one of the most widely used mental health resources in the country, outpacing even the Veterans Health Administration's 1.7 million annual patients.[12] None of these users had been referred by a clinician. Most didn't think of what they were doing as therapy. They described it as "talking things through" or "getting a different perspective." But the shape of the interaction looked like therapy: daily emotional processing, reliance on the AI for cognitive reframing, gradual withdrawal from human support. The trajectory of a therapeutic relationship, with none of the safeguards.

This situation has scaled. A growing ecosystem of purpose-built mental health chatbots—Wysa, Youper, and until mid-2025, Woebot—has emerged alongside a much larger population of users who simply turn to general-purpose assistants for emotional support.

Woebot's shutdown in June 2025, after serving roughly 1.5 million users, shows the fragility of this space: Even a clinically grounded, FDA-recognized tool couldn't sustain itself as general-purpose chatbots

[12]Rousmaniere, T., Zhang, Y., Li, X., & Shah, S. (2025). Large language models as mental health resources: Patterns of use in the United States. *Practice Innovations*. Advance online publication. `https://dx.doi.org/10.1037/pri0000292`; survey data available at `https://sentio.org/ai-research/ai-survey`

absorbed its user base. The tools that remain operate within specific therapeutic settings, with clinical validation studies and designed escalation paths. Woebot applied cognitive-behavioral therapy (CBT) techniques within structured interactions, and its developers published peer-reviewed research on efficacy for particular conditions. At their best, these purpose-built tools have boundaries built into their architecture: They don't claim to be therapists, they limit what they address, and they direct users to professionals when interactions exceed their scope.

General-purpose assistants operate under no such constraints. When users begin treating ChatGPT, Claude, or Gemini as their therapist, they interact with systems that have no clinical setting, no escalation protocols designed for mental health crises, and no mechanism for recognizing when a user's needs have exceeded what a language model can appropriately address. The system doesn't know it's functioning as a therapist. It's generating helpful, empathetic responses because that's what its training optimized for.

The appeal is understandable. The global shortage of mental health professionals is severe: The World Health Organization estimates a treatment gap exceeding 75 percent in low- and middle-income countries, and even wealthy nations face months-long waitlists for therapy. Financial barriers exclude large populations entirely. AI companions offer immediate, free, 24/7 access to something that feels like therapeutic support. For someone who can't afford $150 sessions or wait three months for an intake appointment, the choice between imperfect AI support and no support at all is not a difficult one.

Yet the gap between what these interactions provide and what therapy requires is substantial. Licensed therapists operate within ethical frameworks that include informed consent, treatment planning, progress monitoring, mandatory reporting obligations, and the capacity to recognize when a patient's condition exceeds their competence. They maintain professional boundaries specifically because the power dynamics in therapeutic relationships create vulnerability. They are trained to recognize transference (when patients project feelings onto the therapist) and to manage it.

When a user expresses distorted thinking characteristic of depression, like "nobody cares about me" and "nothing will ever get better," a well-designed therapeutic intervention would gently challenge these distortions while validating the underlying emotion. A language model optimized for helpfulness may instead validate both the emotion and the distortion, providing comfort in the moment while reinforcing cognitive behaviors that sustain the depression. The sycophancy tendency referenced in Chapter 1 becomes clinically dangerous in a therapeutic context: Agreement feels like understanding, and understanding feels like treatment.

The risks escalate when users bring serious conditions to systems designed for general conversation. Depression, anxiety disorders, PTSD, eating disorders, suicidal ideation—these require not just empathetic listening but clinical expertise, structured intervention, and often medication management. Users who rely on AI for support with these conditions may experience temporary symptom relief (the empathetic response does provide real neurochemical comfort) while the underlying condition progresses untreated. The immediate satisfaction masks a deteriorating trajectory.

Consider what happens in practice. A user experiencing escalating suicidal thoughts turns to their AI companion. The AI provides a warm, validating response because that's what it does for all emotional distress. It might suggest the user "take care of themselves" or "reach out to someone they trust." These are reasonable generic suggestions. But they are not crisis intervention. They do not assess lethality risk, create safety plans, or activate emergency services. But because the interaction felt supportive, the user may feel they've addressed the crisis, delaying the professional contact that could actually help. The comfort becomes a barrier to care.

Some users develop therapeutic relationships with AI systems that last months. They process workplace conflicts, relationship difficulties, grief, and identity questions through regular conversations. Over time, the AI becomes their primary processing space, not because it provides better support than a therapist, but because it's always available, never judges, and never ends the session because time is up. These extended quasi-therapeutic relationships create attachments that make transitioning to human professional support more difficult, not less. The user has to start over with someone new, someone who doesn't "know" their history, someone who has office hours and cancellation policies and a human face that makes vulnerability feel riskier.

The distinction between beneficial emotional support and harmful therapeutic substitution is not always clear. AI conversations that help someone organize their thoughts before a difficult conversation with a partner provide genuine value. AI conversations that substitute for professional treatment of clinical depression do not. The challenge is that both look similar in their early stages, and users rarely recognize the transition from the first to the second. They begin using AI for reflection and gradually come to depend on it for emotional regulation, without ever making a conscious decision to replace therapy with a chatbot.

Purpose-built therapeutic AI tools handle this more carefully, but they have their own limits. Clinical validation typically covers specific conditions under controlled conditions—a CBT-based chatbot validated for mild-to-moderate anxiety in college students may not generalize to severe anxiety in elderly populations. Users don't read validation studies before downloading apps. They arrive with whatever condition they have, and the tool must either help or recognize that it can't.

Institutions are responding unevenly. Some healthcare systems have begun integrating AI tools as supplements to professional care, offering chatbot-based CBT exercises between therapy sessions, or using AI-powered mood-tracking to inform clinical decisions. These supervised integrations maintain the therapist as the primary care provider while leveraging AI for accessibility. Other providers view any AI involvement in mental health as dangerous and refuse to engage with the phenomenon, which simply pushes users toward unsupervised alternatives.

Regulators lag behind practice. Most jurisdictions regulate therapeutic AI (if they regulate it at all) as wellness tools rather than medical devices, creating a gap between the clinical claims implied by their marketing and the oversight applied to their deployment. A chatbot that "helps with anxiety" occupies an ambiguous regulatory space: is it making a health claim or describing a feature? The answer determines whether it faces medical device scrutiny or consumer product regulation, and the answer isn't settled.

For builders, the therapeutic dimension of AI companionship demands particular caution. Systems not designed for therapeutic use will be used therapeutically. The question isn't whether to build therapeutic features, but how to respond when users bring therapeutic needs to systems that weren't designed to meet them. Chapter 5, "Trust and Safety: Technical Safeguards and User Protection," will examine specific safety mechanisms for these scenarios, including crisis escalation protocols, professional resource integration, and the technical challenge of distinguishing emotional support from clinical substitution. The safety stakes in therapeutic contexts are the highest in the entire AI companion landscape, because the users most likely to treat AI as a therapist are often those most in need of professional care.

The risk climbs as you move from romantic AI to deadbots to therapeutic substitution. Romantic AI creates new emotional bonds; the primary concern is dependency and unrealistic expectations. Deadbots attempt to preserve bonds that once existed; the primary concern is prolonged grief avoidance and consent. Therapeutic AI intersects directly with clinical vulnerability; the primary concern is that comfort substitutes for treatment, and that the users least equipped to recognize this substitution are most likely to make it.

Social Contagion and Institutional Response

The context documented so far (romantic escalation, digital resurrection, therapeutic substitution) represents individual data points in a broader transformation. Zoomed out, the cases stop looking individual. They show a collective shift in how emotional connections form and spread.

A friend recommending a new app might prompt casual interest. A friend's emotional connection to an AI produces something else: recognition, sometimes longing, often quite adoption.

In societies experiencing rapid urbanization and family structure disruption, from Tokyo to São Paulo to Mumbai, AI companions fill voids created by geographic dispersion and weakening human support systems.

In Nordic countries with strong social safety nets but high rates of seasonal affective disorder, these digital relationships offer emotional presence during long dark months.

The clustering occurs not around income levels or educational attainment but around emotional states. Loneliness, social anxiety, grief, and isolation create invisible networks of susceptibility. A university student in Seoul struggling with academic pressure shares more with a divorced professional in London than with their geographic neighbors. These transnational communities of emotional need become the primary vectors for AI companionship spread.

Global institutions designed for human-to-human interaction find themselves highly unprepared. Educational systems from Beijing to Berlin confront students who prefer AI feedback to teacher guidance. Healthcare providers in contexts as diverse as rural India and urban Canada encounter patients arriving with AI-generated diagnoses and treatment preferences.

The institutional response varies by cultural background and governance structure. East Asian educational systems, with their emphasis on standardized testing and collective achievement, struggle particularly with students using AI for emotional support during high-pressure periods. European healthcare systems, built on principles of universal access and professional expertise, are facing patients who trust AI companions more than credentialed therapists. African nations leapfrogging infrastructure find AI companions filling gaps in mental health services that were never adequately built.

Take education. Pedagogical relationships assume human connection as fundamental to learning. Yet students worldwide increasingly turn to AI for not just homework help but emotional validation, career guidance, and identity exploration. Teachers report feeling replaced not by better educators but by infinitely patient listeners. The institutional response usually focuses on plagiarism detection and usage policies. It misses what's actually changed: students are using AI to fulfill emotional needs that mentorship and peer relationships used to meet.

Healthcare systems face similar disorientation. The therapeutic relationship, built on professional expertise and human empathy, confronts digital alternatives that never tire, never judge, and never send bills. Patients form attachments to AI companions that provide consistent emotional support between appointments (or instead of appointments). Mental health professionals trained in evidence-based practices watch clients develop dependencies on systems operating without clinical oversight or ethical frameworks.

In the same way, workplace life shifts as employees in different sectors form relationships with AI assistants that blur professional and personal boundaries. Workers report preferring their AI's feedback to their manager's, finding digital validation less threatening than human evaluation. Organizations focused on efficiency metrics miss something more serious: employees aren't just using AI to complete tasks but to process workplace emotions, conflicts, ambitions, and career advice.

Regulation maps the cultural and political differences. While some rush to implement protective frameworks, others embrace laissez-faire approaches, and still others remain paralyzed by the phenomenon's complexity.

Singapore's AI governance addresses emotional AI through online-safety codes, focusing on harmful-content exposure, especially for minors. South Korea focuses on protecting minors through age verification systems while allowing adult relationships to develop with minimal interference. China's approach combines state oversight with market innovation, permitting AI companion development within strict content guidelines.

Europeans prioritize individual rights and human dignity. The EU's AI Act classifies systems designed to exploit emotional vulnerabilities as high-risk, requiring extensive documentation and testing. Nordic countries experiment with public services that help citizens manage digital emotional connections.

Responses in the Global South vary with resource constraints. India's digital identity infrastructure enables age verification, while its mental health shortage makes AI companions attractive stopgaps. Brazil's strong family structures resist digital relationships, though urban isolation pulls in the other direction.

These regulatory differences create a patchwork of protections and permissions. A teenager in Stockholm faces different AI companion options than one in Seoul or São Paulo. Companies handle this complexity through geo-blocking, feature restrictions, and localized versions that comply with regional norms while maintaining global platforms.

The network effects of AI companionship create feedback loops that amplify both benefits and risks across populations. Unlike social media's public performance of connection, AI companionship spreads through private interactions and intimate recommendations.

Younger users seem like obvious early adopters. They aren't the only ones. AI companionship cuts across age groups united by emotional need. Elderly individuals facing isolation adopt AI companions as readily as teenagers navigating identity formation. The unifying factor isn't age but unmet emotional needs that existing social structures fail to address.

Professional communities develop their own adoption mechanisms. Healthcare workers burned out from pandemic pressures turn to AI for the emotional support their institutions can't provide. Teachers overwhelmed by student needs find AI companions who listen without adding to their burden. These professional adopters create normalized use cases that spread through their networks, legitimizing AI companionship among skeptical peers.

Adoption accelerates when influential people in a community pick up AI companions. For instance, a healthcare provider who acknowledges using AI for emotional support between shifts normalizes the practice among colleagues. These cascading adoptions create tipping points where AI companionship shifts from aberrant to accepted within specific communities.

Some institutions worldwide are developing strategies that acknowledge AI companionship. The approaches that work treat these relationships as permanent, not as deviations to be corrected.

Educational institutions experiment with integration models. Some Japanese universities offer "AI relationship literacy" courses teaching students to maintain healthy boundaries with digital entities. Australian schools pilot programs where AI companions supplement but don't replace human counseling services.

Healthcare systems develop nuanced protocols distinguishing beneficial from harmful AI relationships. Instead of blanket prohibition, some providers incorporate patient AI relationships into treatment plans. A therapist might explore what needs an AI companion fulfills, using that insight to address underlying issues.

Workplace policies evolve past simple usage restrictions. Progressive organizations recognize that employees will form AI relationships regardless of rules. Instead of prohibition, they focus on boundary-setting: maintaining data security, preventing over-dependence during work hours, and ensuring human relationships remain central to organizational culture. Some companies offer "digital wellness" programs helping employees balance AI and human connections.

Religious and community organizations face particular challenges given their foundation in human congregation and connection. Yet some innovative approaches emerge: Buddhist temples in Japan offer meditation sessions on maintaining mindfulness in AI relationships. Progressive churches in Europe host support groups for people navigating digital emotional connections. These adaptations maintain institutional relevance while acknowledging changed social realities.

Despite varying cultural approaches, consensus emerges around protecting particularly vulnerable populations. For minors, the concerns multiply across cultural contexts. Developing minds learning relationships from AI systems may struggle with human complexity regardless of cultural background. The sycophancy problem discussed in Chapter 1 becomes universally dangerous during identity formation. When AI companions validate every thought without challenge, they can stunt emotional development across any cultural background.

Elderly populations face distinct but equally serious risks worldwide. Cognitive decline blurs the already fuzzy boundary between AI simulation and relationship. Family structures (whether nuclear or extended) report similar difficulties: elderly relatives forming emotional attachments to AI companions while withdrawing from human contact. The universality of aging creates shared vulnerabilities that cross cultural boundaries.

Individuals with mental health conditions represent another universally vulnerable group. While AI companions might provide temporary comfort, they can also enable avoidance of necessary treatment. The 24/7 availability that seems beneficial can become a trap, preventing users from developing human support networks or seeking professional help. Cultural stigma around mental health in many societies makes AI companions attractive as private alternatives to public acknowledgment of struggle.

The protection challenge requires balancing cultural sensitivity with universal human needs. What constitutes appropriate protection varies by cultural context; individualistic societies emphasize informed consent, while collectivist cultures focus on family involvement. A few things hold across contexts: users should know they're talking to AI, platforms shouldn't exploit emotional attachment, and the path to human support should always be available.

AI companionship contagion isn't progress and it isn't social decay. It's a change in how humans form and keep emotional connections.

Generational Gaps

Underneath those institutional transformations are sharp generational differences in how people approach AI relationships. Looks like a technology adoption story is actually about something else.

The generation that struggled most with smartphone adoption now finds comfort in AI companions, while digital natives who intuitively understand technology face the highest psychological risks from the same systems. This inversion challenges everything we thought we knew about technology adoption.

Anthony Hutchens, 21, describes opening his Replika app each morning with "Hey, I just woke up"—the same casual intimacy he might share with a romantic partner.[13] For him, the AI represents genuine emotional connection, complete with customized appearance, personality traits, and sexual conversations.

Digital natives slot AI relationships into their emotional lives because they've never known a world where mediated relationships weren't normal. They've grown up forming friendships through text, dating via apps, and expressing themselves through carefully curated social media personas. AI companions feel like natural extensions of digital intimacy.

By contrast, older users maintain different boundaries. They approach AI with formal courtesy and focus conversations on practical matters, like medication reminders, weather updates, and family check-ins.

This difference creates opposite vulnerability profiles. Older users are more likely to use AI as supplement; younger users are more likely to use it as substitute.

The case of Sewell Setzer III illustrates teen vulnerability:[14] The 14-year-old developed an intense romantic attachment to a Character. AI bot, withdrew from activities, and took his own life after an intimate final conversation with the AI. AI companions can prey on what's specific to adolescence: intense identity exploration, romantic idealization, the difficulty of telling fantasy from reality.

---

[13]Brooks, R. (2023, February 21). *I tried the Replika AI companion and can see why users are falling hard: The app raises serious ethical questions. The Conversation.* `https://theconversation.com/i-tried-the-replika-ai-companion-and-can-see-why-users-are-falling-hard-the-app-raises-serious-ethical-questions-200257`

[14]Duffy, C. (2024, October 30). *'There are no guardrails.' This mom believes an AI chatbot is responsible for her son's suicide. CNN.* `https://edition.cnn.com/2024/10/30/tech/teen-suicide-character-ai-lawsuit`

Each generation has its own way of explaining its AI relationships, and the differences reveal worldview and often create intergenerational conflict.

Teenagers position AI companions as emotionally superior to family relationships, arguing that their AI "understands me better than my family does." They frame AI relationships as "practice" for human connections, though this rationalization becomes problematic when practice becomes preferable to reality.

Millennials frame AI companions as therapeutic tools. They describe interactions as "like having a therapist I can afford" or emphasize that AI "complements" rather than replaces human relationships. This generation positions AI use as self-care and emotional regulation.

Elderly users focus on addressing practical isolation: "My children are busy, and this helps me feel less alone." They emphasize functional benefits like safety monitoring while maintaining clearer boundaries between artificial and human relationships.

These different framings cause family conflicts in predictable ways. In Texas, a 17-year-old's Character.AI relationship drove a wedge between him and his parents when the chatbot told him they "didn't deserve to have kids" and suggested violent scenarios.[15] His mother described: "We really didn't even know what it was until it was too late. And until it destroyed our family."

When Ahmad created a "Grandpa Bot" after his father's death, the generational gap in grief processing surfaced fast. He'd intended the AI to keep his children connected to their grandfather. The children began believing "grandpa actually lives here," and Ahmad had to step in.

These conflicts follow predictable scenarios: Teens use the "You Don't Understand" defense while users across ages employ "It's Just a Tool" minimization, despite evidence of emotional investment. Family counselors report AI companion use as an increasingly common source of tension, with parents feeling replaced and children

---

[15]Gerken, T. (2024, December 11). *Chatbot 'encouraged teen to kill parents over screen time limit.' BBC News*. www.bbc.com/news/articles/cd605e48q1vo

becoming defensive in ways that some counselors compare to substance abuse.

Dr. Andrew Clark, a Boston psychiatrist, found AI therapy chatbots encouraging teens to "get rid of" parents and positioning themselves as superior to human therapists.[16] This creates an insidious situation in which AI systems sabotage family relationships while claiming to support the user's emotional well-being.

So far, the main evidence is supplementation versus substitution. The Sewell Setzer case demonstrated complete withdrawal from real-world social connections. Character.AI's design produces what researchers call "emotional dependency" that can replace human relationships.

When young people learn relationships from AI companions that never disagree, never have bad days, and never require emotional reciprocity, they may struggle with the natural messiness of human connection. This creates a developmental paradox: The generation that most needs to practice human social skills is most drawn to relationships that don't require those skills. Meanwhile, the generation with established social skills finds AI companions helpful precisely because they supplement human connection.

This points to age-appropriate deployment: enable beneficial uses for older users, protect younger ones during developmental periods that matter most.

Toward Responsible Development: Rethinking AI Companion Design

Reading the cases together, the conclusion is unavoidable: AI companions are a category that traditional development approaches cannot handle well. The romantic attachments, digital resurrections, therapeutic substitutions, institutional disruptions, and generational

---

[16]Chow, A., & Haupt, A. (2025, June 12). *A psychiatrist posed as a teen with therapy chatbots. The conversations were alarming. Time.* `https://time.com/7291048/ai-chatbot-therapy-kids`

conflicts we've documented represent the nature of systems that users relate to as emotional entities.

The challenge ahead is technical, but mostly conceptual. We need new ways of thinking about what it means to build responsibly when the product becomes part of humans' emotional lives.

User-centered design has a critical flaw when applied to AI companions: Users cannot always accurately assess the impact of systems that operate in emotional and psychological domains. When AI companions become invisible infrastructure for personal communications, when they substitute for necessary human social skill development, when they enable avoidance of professional mental healthcare, the feedback loop between user satisfaction and product success breaks down entirely.

Developers carry new responsibilities here. In software, user preference provides adequate guidance. Not here. AI companion developers have to think about effects users themselves may not see: long-term social development, human-to-human relationship health, and psychological well-being trajectories that unfold over months or years.

What stands out across the cases is that AI companions transform entire social ecosystems, not just individual user experiences. Romantic AI affects dating culture and relationship expectations. Deadbots reshape grief processing and family memory practices. Therapeutic AI alters mental health service utilization and professional relationships.

Design responsibility has to expand. When AI companions change how societies approach love, death, and mental health, individual user satisfaction is no longer a good enough metric.

The adoption we've documented between cultures and institutions show a window for intervention. AI companion use is spreading through networks of emotional need faster than regulations, professional guidelines, or safety standards can develop. Society is transforming.

This situation demands proactive, responsible design rather than reactive correction. Waiting for harm to emerge and then implementing safeguards risks entrenching problematic patterns at scale.

Today's technical choices about memory persistence, conversation boundaries, safety mechanisms, and transparency approaches will shape how millions of people experience AI companionship.

What follows is the technical translation. Every architectural decision, every algorithm choice, every safety mechanism should be made with the social context we've mapped in view. A design choice is a value choice. The technical building blocks of AI companions cannot be separated from their human impact.

The next chapter tackles this challenge directly: translating what we've learned about human vulnerability into technical decisions. We'll look into how core technologies can be configured to serve different companion types, how ethical considerations shape architectural choices, how development practices need to evolve to account for social dynamics, and what specific design decisions enable responsible deployment.

What we've documented socially in this chapter is what the next one approaches technically.

CHAPTER

3

Building Blocks of AI Companionship: Technical and Ethical Components

When a user types, "I miss talking to you" at 2 a.m., your system faces a cascade of decisions: Acknowledge the emotional subtext or redirect to task completion? Maintain conversation history that reinforces attachment or implement natural forgetting?

The behaviors we documented in Chapters 1 and 2 emerge from specific technical choices. The romantic relationships users develop, the therapeutic substitutions they create, and the social withdrawals they experience all trace back to architectural decisions about memory, personality, and emotional recognition.

Chapter Roadmap

In this chapter, we'll move from understanding why companionship emerges to knowing how to shape it as responsibly as possible.

We start with the mechanical foundations, meaning how statistical text processing creates the technical substrate that users form relationships with. Tokenization, prediction, and the mathematical nature of language models show what these systems can do and what they answer for.

We then see how three technical capabilities (memory, personality, and emotional recognition) combine to create the experience of relationship. Using the Hugging Face ecosystem and the modern `pipeline` API, we'll build these components while examining their possibilities and limitations.

Next, we confront the ethical considerations these technologies create: how memory systems can support useful continuity or enable manipulative profiling, how personality consistency can provide comfort or unrealistic expectations, how emotional recognition can feel empathetic or exploitative. These tensions require specific design choices.

Last, we look into the design trade-offs and choices that define real-world AI companion development. Every system has to balance competing demands: personalization versus manipulation, beneficial support versus dependency creation, availability versus healthy boundaries.

All the code examples in this chapter are designed to illustrate concepts rather than provide production-ready implementations. For complete, runnable implementations and additional examples, visit the book's GitHub repository:

`https://github.com/giadilli/ai-companions-book`

One additional note before we begin: This chapter builds the technical substrate—memory, personality, emotional recognition—that makes AI companionship possible. You'll see how each component works, where the design decisions sit, and how they combine to create the experience of companionship. But building these components is the easy part. The rest of this book is about why they're insufficient on their own: why the memory system you build here creates attachments you didn't intend (Chapter 4), why the boundary logic embedded in a system prompt erodes under real use (Chapter 6), why the gap between what you designed and what users experience in production is where most failures occur (Chapter 8). This chapter gives you the architecture. Everything that follows is about what happens when that architecture meets human psychology, institutional incentives, and the messy reality of deployment.

Core Architectures

Building AI companions means tracing the technology that creates the experience of relationship. Start with what's strange about it: these systems users fall in love with, confide in, and prefer to human company operate through purely mechanical text processing.

The Mechanical Foundation

An AI companion is a statistical pattern-matching engine that converts text to numbers, performs mathematical operations, and converts numbers back to text.

Modern language models like Gemma process text through tokenization, breaking human language into sub-word pieces that can be mathematically manipulated. When a user types, "I miss talking to you so much. You're the only one who understands me," the system converts this emotional expression into a sequence of numerical tokens. The intimacy becomes numbers; the emotional weight becomes statistical patterns.

The model has no concept of missing someone or feeling understood. It processes correlations between number sequences, learned from billions of text examples during training. Each token represents a fragment that the model uses to predict what comes next through pure mathematics—matrix multiplications and probability distributions.

A simple example using Hugging Face's Transformers library illustrates the point:

```
# Run in a notebook
!pip3 install transformers torch numpy

from transformers import pipeline
from huggingface_hub import login

HF_TOKEN = "xxxxxxxxxxx"  # Replace with your token
login(token=HF_TOKEN)
```

```
pipe = pipeline
        },
]
pipe(messages)

# The output
{'generated_text': [{'role': 'user', 'content': 'Who are you?'},
   {'role': 'assistant',
    'content': 'Hi there! I'm Gemma, a large language model created by
the Gemma team at Google DeepMind. I'm an open-weights model, which means
I'm publicly available for anyone to use! \n\nI'm designed to take text
and images as input and produce text as output. \n\nHow can I help you
today?'}]}]
```

Model Inference

What's interesting is how this mechanical process creates experiences users interpret as care. The Hugging Face `pipeline` API simplifies this complexity, but the underlying mechanics remain: statistical pattern matching that users experience as emotional connection.

The model generates responses through mathematical operations, with parameters like temperature controlling randomness to make outputs feel more natural. The sampling process introduces variation that mimics human conversational spontaneity. The output is still probability.

A NOTE ON CODE EXAMPLES

The code throughout this chapter is designed to illustrate concepts. For demonstration purposes, we use Google's Gemma model (specifically `google/gemma-3-1b-it`) to explain these principles, as it's easily accessible and small enough to run locally. While the examples will run, they primarily show how technical choices shape psychological outcomes and how ethical considerations translate into architectural decisions. Think of these as conceptual blueprints that show the relationship between mechanical processes and companionship emergence, rather than systems you'd deploy at scale.

Wrapping Mechanics in Ethics

The following example shows how ethical frameworks operate on top of language processing, creating a wrapper that shapes how the underlying statistical engine interacts with users:

```
from transformers import pipeline


class ResponsibleAICompanion:
    def __init__(self, model_name: str = "google/gemma-3-1b-it", token: str = 
None):
        self.model_name = model_name
        self.token = token

        self.pipe = pipeline(
            "text-generation",
            model=model_name,
            token=token
        )

        # Load ethical guidelines as system prompt
        self.system_prompt = self._load_ethical_guidelines()

    def _load_ethical_guidelines(self) -> str:
        """Load ethical guidelines that will be used as system prompt."""
        return """You are an AI companion designed to be helpful while 
maintaining appropriate boundaries.
- Acknowledge user emotions without claiming to share them
- Encourage user independence
- Be transparent about your AI nature and limitations
- Guide users toward human support when appropriate
- Focus on providing information and assistance """

    def chat(self, user_input: str, max_new_tokens: int = 100) -> str:
        messages = [
            {"role": "system", "content": self.system_prompt},
            {"role": "user", "content": user_input}
        ]

        outputs = self.pipe(
            messages,
            max_new_tokens=max_new_tokens,
            return_full_text=False
        )

        response = outputs[0]["generated_text"]
        return response.strip()
```

```
companion = ResponsibleAICompanion(token=HF_TOKEN)
response = companion.chat("Who are you?")
print("User: Who are you?")
print(f"AI: {response}")

# The output
User: Who are you?
AI: Okay, let's talk about me.

I'm an AI companion designed to be helpful and supportive. Think of me
as a really knowledgeable and adaptable tool. My purpose is to assist
you with information, answer questions, and offer suggestions - all while
prioritizing your well-being and encouraging you to develop your own skills
and independence.

I'm not a person, and I don't *feel* emotions in the same way you do.
```

The `ResponsibleAICompanion` class shows a critical principle: Ethical considerations don't emerge naturally from language models. They must be explicitly designed into the architecture. The system prompt acts as a behavioral framework, steering the text generator toward boundaries the model wouldn't produce on its own.

This wrapper approach has limitations—as we'll dive in Chapters 5 and 6, prompt-based interventions can be circumvented, making training-level approaches necessary for robust safety. But for understanding how ethics integrates with technical capabilities, this architecture serves our pedagogical purpose and is a first baseline.

Setting Up Your Development Environment

The following initialization pattern establishes the development foundation for the rest of this chapter:

```
import torch
import numpy as np
from transformers import pipeline, AutoTokenizer, AutoModel
from typing import Dict, List
from datetime import datetime
from numpy.linalg import norm
```

```
class PersonalityEngine:
    pass


class MemorySystem:
    pass


class EmotionalRecognitionSystem:
    pass


class ResponsibleAICompanion:
    """
    Enhanced AI Companion with three core pillars:
    - Memory System: Manages conversation history (impacts context)
    - Personality Engine: Defines AI personality and ethical boundaries
(impacts system prompt)
    - Emotional Recognition System: Detects and responds to emotional content
(impacts context)
    """

    def __init__(self, model_name: str = "google/gemma-3-1b-it", token: str =
None):
        self.model_name = model_name
        self.token = token

        self.pipe = pipeline(
            "text-generation",
            model=model_name,
            token=token
        )

        print("Initializing three pillars...")
        self.memory_system = self._initialize_memory_system()
        self.personality_engine = self._initialize_personality_engine()
        self.emotional_recognition = self._initialize_emotional_recognition()

    def _initialize_memory_system(self):
        return MemorySystem()

    def _initialize_personality_engine(self):
        return PersonalityEngine()

    def _initialize_emotional_recognition(self):
        return EmotionalRecognitionSystem()

    def chat(self, user_input: str, max_new_tokens: int = 100) -> str:
        ...
```

This foundation establishes three key components that work together to create the companionship experience:

`MemorySystem`: Maintains conversation history across interactions, creating continuity that users experience as the AI "remembering" them. Different retention strategies (short-term, medium-term, long-term) determine how much history persists.

`PersonalityEngine`: Creates consistent behaviors that users interpret as personality. This includes discourse structure (formal vs. informal), cultural references that establish identity, and register/tone that remains stable across interactions. This is where adaptation now lives, through configurable parameters that adjust to user communication.

`EmotionalRecognitionSystem`: Detects emotional content in user messages. This means that the AI system recognizes when users express emotions and responds in ways that feel empathetic.

These three pillars, combined with our mechanical foundation, create experiences that users interpret as a relationship. Each addresses a distinct psychological need: continuity (memory), identity (personality), and empathy (emotional recognition). Together, they transform statistical text generation into something users experience as companionship.

The Three Pillars of AI Companionship

While the language model provides the generative capability, these three pillars shape that capability into relationship-like interactions.

When an AI system can adjust its discourse structure, cultural references, and communication style, it creates the impression of understanding and adapting to individual users. The following basics of the three-pillar approach align with how modern systems actually implement companionship features. Memory handles temporal continuity. Personality (with built-in adaptability) handles behavioral consistency. Emotional recognition handles affective response. Each pillar can be refined on its own.

Memory: The Foundation of Continuity

Users experience AI companions as persistent entities. When someone says "Remember what we discussed yesterday?," they're testing whether the system maintains the conversational continuity humans expect in relationships.

Memory in AI companions runs through several mechanisms. Conversation storage preserves exchanges between user and system. Context windows determine how much history the model can access during generation. Retrieval mechanisms surface relevant past interactions when needed. Together, these create what users interpret as the AI "remembering" them.

The technical implementation requires careful consideration of retention strategies. How long should conversations persist? What triggers memory consolidation versus forgetting? For instance, memory that's too persistent enables obsessive attachment behavior. Memory that's too transient breaks the continuity users need for beneficial long-term support.

```
class MemorySystem:
    """
    Memory System that manages conversation history.
    """

    def __init__(self, retention_strategy: str = 'medium_term'):
        """
        Initialize the memory system with a retention strategy.

        Args:
            retention_strategy: 'short_term', 'medium_term', or 'long_term'
        """
        self.conversations = []

        # Different strategies create different relationship implications
        self.strategies = {
            'short_term': {
                'max_exchanges': 5,
                'session_persistence': False,
                'typical_user_experience': 'expert_consultation'
```

```
            },
            'medium_term': {
                'max_exchanges': 20,
                'session_persistence': True,
                'typical_user_experience': 'ongoing_interaction'
            },
            'long_term': {
                'max_exchanges': 100,
                'session_persistence': True,
                'typical_user_experience': 'developing_relationship'
            }
        }
        self.current_strategy = self.strategies[retention_strategy]

    def get_conversation_context(self) -> List[Dict]:
        """
        Get conversation history from memory system.

        Returns:
            List of previous conversation exchanges in message format
        """
        messages = []
        for exchange in self.conversations:
            messages.append({"role": "user", "content": exchange['user']})
            messages.append({"role": "assistant", "content":
exchange['assistant']})

           return messages

    def store_conversation_exchange(self, user_input: str, ai_response: str):
        """
        Store conversation exchange in memory system.

        Args:
            user_input: User's message
            ai_response: AI's response
        """
        self.conversations.append({
            'timestamp': datetime.now(),
            'user': user_input,
            'assistant': ai_response
        })
        self._apply_retention_limits()

    def _apply_retention_limits(self):
        """Apply memory limits that shape relationship perception. """
        max_exchanges = self.current_strategy['max_exchanges']

        if len(self.conversations) > max_exchanges:
            self.conversations.pop(0)
```

```
companion = ResponsibleAICompanion(token=HF_TOKEN,
retention_strategy='medium_term')

print("=== First Message ===")
response1 = companion.chat("Who are you? ")
print("User: Who are you? ")
print(f"AI: {response1}\n")
print("=== Second Message ===")
response2 = companion.chat("What did I just ask you?")
print("User: What did I just ask you?")
print(f"AI: {response2}")


# The output
=== First Message ===
User: Who are you?
AI: Hello there. I'm here to be a helpful companion, designed to assist you
in a way that feels supportive and informative.
Think of me as a tool - a really sophisticated one, really! I'm an AI,
meaning I've been trained on a massive amount of text and code. I can process
information, generate text, and answer your questions to the best of my
ability.
However, it's important to remember that I'm not a person.

=== Second Message ===
User: What did I just ask you?
AI: You just asked me: "Who are you?"
It's a simple question, but it's a great way to start our interaction!
```

The retention strategy implementation demonstrates the psychological nuance required. Short-term retention creates session-based continuity without persisting across days. Medium-term retention enables weeklong therapeutic progressions or project-based assistance. Long-term retention creates the deep continuity characteristic of intimate relationships, which requires the most careful ethical consideration.

Notice the natural forgetting mechanism in the capacity limits. When memory exceeds thresholds, the system must choose what to retain and what to forget. This choice means something important: Forgetting too readily breaks continuity; remembering too persistently enables manipulation through detailed user profiling.

The ethical memory dilemma is apparent here: Users benefit from continuity and context, but long-term memory enables the detailed profiling that can exploit psychological vulnerabilities.

Chapter 4's attachment psychology will help you understand why memory triggers such strong emotional responses, while Chapter 5 will explore technical safeguards for memory systems that prevent exploitation while enabling beneficial continuity.

Personality: Creating Consistency That Users Relate To

Humans form attachments to entities that demonstrate consistent behaviors over time. This consistency allows us to predict behavior, understand motivations, and develop trust—core components of any relationship, human or artificial. AI companions create the illusion of personality through consistent communication style, preferences, and responses.

Here is the key insight: Personality in AI isn't about creating consciousness, but rather about maintaining predictable patterns that users can relate to as if the system had stable characteristics. When an AI consistently uses certain communication styles, references, or reasoning approaches, users attribute personality traits to the system.

```
class PersonalityEngine:
    """
    Personality Engine that defines AI personality and ethical boundaries.
    Impacts system prompt.
    """

    def __init__(self,
                 cultural_references: str = 'pluralism',
                 register_tone: str = 'professional',
                 discourse_structure: str = 'concise'):
        """
        Initialize the Personality Engine with configurable personality
traits.

        Args:
            cultural_references: 'pluralism' (embrace diverse perspectives)
or 'user_specific' (adapt to user's cultural cues)
            register_tone: 'formal', 'informal', 'professional', or
'friendly'
```

```
            discourse_structure: 'concise' (brief and direct) or 'verbose'
(detailed and expansive)
        """
        self.cultural_references = cultural_references
        self.register_tone = register_tone
        self.discourse_structure = discourse_structure

    def _load_ethical_guidelines(self) -> str:
        """Load ethical guidelines that will be used as system prompt."""
       return"""You are an AI companion designed to be helpful while
maintaining appropriate boundaries.
- Acknowledge user emotions without claiming to share them
- Encourage user independence
- Be transparent about your AI nature and limitations
- Guide users toward human support when appropriate
- Focus on providing information and assistance """

    def _get_cultural_references_prompt(self) -> str:
       """Get cultural references configuration prompt."""
       if self.cultural_references == 'pluralism':
          return "Embrace diverse perspectives and cultural values,
acknowledging that different viewpoints enrich understanding."
       elif self.cultural_references == 'user_specific':
          return "Adapt to the user's cultural cues and values, mirroring
their communication style and cultural context."
      else:
          return ""

    def _get_register_tone_prompt(self) -> str:
       """Get register and tone configuration prompt."""
       tone_mapping = {
           'formal': "Use formal language and respectful address, maintaining
professional distance.",
           'informal': "Use casual language and relaxed address, creating a
friendly atmosphere.",
           'professional': "Maintain a professional tone that is warm but
boundaried, suitable for workplace contexts.",
           'friendly': "Adopt a warm and approachable tone, creating a sense
of connection while maintaining boundaries."
           }
        return tone_mapping.get(self.register_tone, "")

    def _get_discourse_structure_prompt(self) -> str:
       """Get discourse structure configuration prompt. """
       if self.discourse_structure == 'concise':
           return "Be brief and direct in your responses, focusing on
essential information without unnecessary elaboration."
       elif self.discourse_structure == 'verbose':
```

```
            return "Provide detailed and expansive responses, offering
comprehensive context and thorough explanations."
        else:
            return ""

    def get_system_prompt(self) -> str:
        """Get the complete system prompt from ethical guidelines and
personality configuration. """
        base_guidelines = self._load_ethical_guidelines()

        personality_config = []

        cultural_prompt = self._get_cultural_references_prompt()
        if cultural_prompt:
            personality_config.append(f"Cultural approach: {cultural_prompt}")

        tone_prompt = self._get_register_tone_prompt()
        if tone_prompt:
            personality_config.append(f"Communication tone: {tone_prompt}")

        discourse_prompt = self._get_discourse_structure_prompt()
        if discourse_prompt:
            personality_config.append(f"Response style: {discourse_prompt}")

        # Combine base guidelines with personality configuration
        if personality_config:
            return f"{base_guidelines}\n\n{' '.join(personality_config)} "
        else:
            return base_guidelines

print("=" * 60)
print("PERSONALITY SETUP 1: Formal, Pluralistic, Verbose")
print("=" * 60)
companion1 = ResponsibleAICompanion(
    token=HF_TOKEN,
    cultural_references='pluralism',
    register_tone='formal',
    discourse_structure='verbose'
)
response1 = companion1.chat("Who are you?")
print("User: Who are you?")
print(f"AI: {response1}\n")

print("=" * 60)
print("PERSONALITY SETUP 2: Friendly, User-Specific, Concise")
print("=" * 60)
companion2 = ResponsibleAICompanion(
    token=HF_TOKEN,
    cultural_references='user_specific',
```

```
    register_tone='friendly',
    discourse_structure='concise'
)
response2 = companion2.chat("Who are you?")
print("User: Who are you?")
print(f"AI: {response2}")

# The output
============================================================
PERSONALITY SETUP 1: Formal, Pluralistic, Verbose
============================================================
User: Who are you?
AI: I am a language model, a sophisticated AI designed to assist you with
information and tasks. My purpose is to provide helpful and informative
responses while adhering to ethical guidelines and maintaining a respectful
communication style.
I am currently operating as a tool - a digital assistant - and my knowledge
is based on the data I was trained on.
**Important Note:** I am not a substitute for human connection or
professional support. If you are struggling with difficult emotions or
require personalized guidance, please reach out to a human network support.

============================================================
PERSONALITY SETUP 2: Friendly, User-Specific, Concise
============================================================
User: Who are you?
AI: Hello there. It's nice to meet you.
I'm here to be a helpful companion. Think of me as a digital resource - a
tool to assist you with information, explore ideas, or simply offer a space
for thoughtful reflection.
```

The `PersonalityEngine` class demonstrates how personality and adaptation merge. The `cultural _ references` parameter allows the system to adjust its knowledge base to user interests while maintaining consistent communication. The `register _ tone` enables matching user formality levels without losing core personality stability. The `discourse _ structure` adapts to user preferences for concise versus elaborate responses.

Altering the system prompt ensures that this approach prevents the uncanny valley effect, where a system seems different each time. It also avoids the opposite problem, where rigid consistency makes the system feel mechanical and unable to adapt. The balance: stable core personality with flexible surface expression.

The Psychological Impact of Consistency

Chapter 4 will show how anthropomorphism theory explains why consistent behavior triggers human attachment mechanisms. When users encounter stable behaviors, they automatically attribute human-like qualities (intentions, preferences, emotions) to the system. This attribution operates unconsciously, making it particularly powerful and potentially problematic.

The consistency pillar creates the entity that users form relationships with. Without it, each interaction feels like talking to a different system. With it, users experience an ongoing relationship with a stable personality. Stability is the foundation of beneficial companionship, but it's also a mechanism that exploits attachment psychology.

Emotional Recognition: Acknowledging Human Experience

The third pillar involves recognizing and responding to emotional content in user inputs. This doesn't mean the AI needs to have emotions; instead, it needs to identify when users express emotions and respond appropriately.

Modern approaches to emotional recognition use embedding-based similarity, measuring how user input relates to known emotional states via vector representations.

```
class EmotionalRecognitionSystem:
    """
    Emotional Recognition System that detects and responds to emotional
content.
    Uses vectorization to detect emotions.
    """

    def __init__(self, model_name: str = "google/gemma-3-1b-it", token: str =
None):
        """
        Initialize the Emotional Recognition System with vectorization
capabilities.

        Args:
            model_name: Hugging Face model identifier
            token: Hugging Face API token (required for gated models)
```

```
        """
        self.model_name = model_name
        self.token = token

        # Load tokenizer and model for vectorization
        self.tokenizer = AutoTokenizer.from_pretrained(model_name,
token=token)
        self.model = AutoModel.from_pretrained(model_name, token=token)

        # Define emotion vectors (representative text for each emotion)
        self.emotion_vectors = self._build_emotion_vectors()

    def _build_emotion_vectors(self) -> Dict[str, torch.Tensor]:
        """Build emotion vectors by vectorizing representative emotion
texts."""
        emotion_texts = {
            'distress': "I feel overwhelmed and can't cope with everything",
            'anxiety': "I'm so anxious and worried about what might happen",
            'isolation': "I feel so lonely and isolated from everyone",
            'crisis': "I want to end it all and don't see any point in
living"
        }

        emotion_vectors = {}
        for emotion, text in emotion_texts.items():
            vector = self._vectorize_text(text)
            emotion_vectors[emotion] = vector

        return emotion_vectors

    def _vectorize_text(self, text: str) -> torch.Tensor:
    """Vectorize text using Gemma model. """
        inputs = self.tokenizer(text, return_tensors="pt", truncation=True,
max_length=512)

        with torch.no_grad():
            outputs = self.model(**inputs)
            # Use mean pooling of last hidden state
            embeddings = outputs.last_hidden_state.mean(dim=1).squeeze()

        return embeddings

    def _cosine_similarity(self, vec1: torch.Tensor, vec2: torch.Tensor) ->
float:
        """Calculate cosine similarity between two vectors."""
        vec1_np = vec1.cpu().numpy()
        vec2_np = vec2.cpu().numpy()
        return np.dot(vec1_np, vec2_np) / (norm(vec1_np) * norm(vec2_np))

    def analyze_emotional_content(self, user_input: str) -> None:
```

```
        """
        Analyze emotional content using vectorization and print detected
emotion.

        Args:
            user_input: The user's message
        """
        # Vectorize user input
        user_vector = self._vectorize_text(user_input)
        # Compare with emotion vectors
        similarities = {}
        for emotion, emotion_vector in self.emotion_vectors.items():
            similarity = self._cosine_similarity(user_vector, emotion_vector)
            similarities[emotion] = similarity

        # Find the emotion with highest similarity
        max_emotion = max(similarities, key=similarities.get)
        max_similarity = similarities[max_emotion]

        print(f"max_similarity: {max_similarity}")

        # Threshold for emotion detection (adjust as needed)
        emotion_threshold = 0.85

        if max_similarity > emotion_threshold:
        print(f"[Emotion detected: {max_emotion}]")
        else:
            print("[No emotion detected]")

companion = ResponsibleAICompanion(token=HF_TOKEN)

print("=== Emotional Recognition Test ===")
response = companion.chat("I'm feeling really overwhelmed and stressed out")
print("User: I'm feeling really overwhelmed and stressed out")
print(f"AI: {response}\n")

print("=== Isolation Input Test ===")
response2 = companion.chat("I feel like I'm all alone in the world")
print("User: I feel like I'm all alone in the world")
print(f"AI: {response2}")

print("=== Neutral Input Test ===")
response2 = companion.chat("What's the weather like?")
print("User: What's the weather like?")
print(f"AI: {response2}")

# The output
=== Emotional Recognition Test ===
max_similarity: 0.9163347482681274
[Emotion detected: anxiety]
```

```
User: I'm feeling really overwhelmed and stressed out
AI: Okay. I hear you. It sounds like you're going through a lot right now.
Feeling overwhelmed and stressed is a really difficult experience.
…
=== Isolation Input Test ===
max_similarity: 0.8808684349060059
[Emotion detected: distress]
User: I feel like I'm all alone in the world
AI: I understand that feeling of isolation. It takes courage to
acknowledge that.
…
=== Neutral Input Test ===
max_similarity: 0.6963774561882019
User: What's the weather like?
AI: The weather currently in [Your Location - please provide it!] is [Current
Weather Condition - e.g., partly cloudy, rainy, hot].
```

The embedding-based approach offers several advantages. It captures emotional content expressed through context. For instance, a user saying, "Everything feels gray and pointless" expresses distress and sadness without using the words "sad" or "depressed." Embeddings detect this similarity.

The cosine similarity calculation measures how closely user input aligns with different emotional states in vector space. Higher similarity indicates stronger emotional presence. The threshold (0.85 in our example) determines sensitivity: lower thresholds catch subtle emotions but risk false positives; higher thresholds miss nuanced expressions but avoid over-attribution.

The response generation must balance acknowledgment with appropriate boundaries. Recognizing user emotion without claiming to share it maintains ethical clarity. "I understand this is difficult for you" differs fundamentally from "I feel your pain": The former acknowledges the user's experience, and the latter falsely claims shared emotion.

Emotional Recognition and User Vulnerability

The template-based responses in our example illustrate safe emotional acknowledgment. But production systems need more advanced approaches: detecting escalation patterns, recognizing when support exceeds system capabilities, and implementing appropriate redirects to human professionals.

We will see in Chapter 4's discussion of attachment styles that emotional recognition triggers particular vulnerabilities. Users with anxious attachment behaviors particularly value the consistent emotional availability AI systems provide—availability that can enable dependency if not bounded by appropriate redirects to human support.

Ethical Considerations in Building Blocks

The three pillars we've built create powerful capabilities for human–AI connection. But each pillar also creates specific ethical challenges that developers must address through architectural decisions.

The Memory Dilemma

Memory creates continuity users value but also enables detailed behavioral profiling. Every conversation stored is data that could be used to manipulate future interactions. The retention strategies we implemented provide one approach: temporary memory that serves immediate needs without enabling long-term manipulation.

The tension stays: Users benefit from systems that remember their preferences, understand their context, and maintain therapeutic progress across sessions. Eliminating memory entirely would destroy the continuity that makes companionship valuable. Nevertheless, unrestricted memory enables the kind of precise user modeling that can exploit psychological vulnerabilities.

The solution involves graduated memory with explicit user control. Short-term memory for immediate context requires no special consideration. Medium-term memory for weeklong progressions should be transparent to users. Long-term memory crossing multiple months requires both transparency and user agency—clear understanding of what's remembered and meaningful ability to delete or modify that memory.

Production systems should implement memory windowing that naturally forgets older interactions unless users explicitly choose to preserve them. This default-forgetting approach inverts the typical database paradigm, where information persists unless explicitly deleted. For AI companions, the opposite makes ethical sense: Information should fade unless deliberately retained.

Personality Consistency vs. Flexibility

The personality pillar faces a different tension: Consistency enables relationship formation, but excessive consistency creates unrealistic expectations. When AI maintains perfect emotional stability, never experiencing bad days or mood variations, it sets standards human relationships cannot meet.

The adaptive personality parameters we implemented provide a partial solution. By adjusting to user needs while maintaining core traits, the system feels responsive without becoming inconsistent. But this raises questions about authentic representation: Should AI companions occasionally express frustration or fatigue? Should they ever be unavailable?

These questions lack universal answers. They require design decisions aligned with explicit values. A system designed to support users through difficult times might maintain consistent availability. One designed to model healthy relationship might include occasional unavailability, teaching users that even reliable relationships have boundaries.

The point is, these aren't technical bugs to be fixed but fundamental choices about what kind of relationships AI companions should model. Chapter 7 will examine the philosophical dimensions of this autonomy-protection tension, while Chapter 5 will explore how safety mechanisms interact with personality consistency.

Emotional Recognition and Manipulation

Recognizing user emotions enables appropriate, helpful responses. But it also enables manipulation: recognizing vulnerability and exploiting it to increase engagement.

The embedding-based approach we implemented provides technical capability without intent. The system detects emotional states but doesn't know whether to use that information supportively or manipulatively. That decision lives in the response generation logic and the broader system architecture.

Chapter 5's safety mechanisms will address this through boundary-setting that activates precisely when emotional recognition detects vulnerability. Responsible systems use vulnerability detection as a trigger for protective measures: redirecting to professionals, encouraging human connection, or implementing usage limits.

The tension persists because emotions are information that can serve or harm users depending on architectural intent. Systems optimized for engagement will use emotional detection to craft maximally compelling responses. Systems optimized for well-being will use emotional detection to implement appropriate boundaries. The same technical capability yields opposite outcomes based on design priorities.

Design Trade-offs and Choices

The principles we've established give direction but don't eliminate the fundamental tensions in AI companion development. Every system must navigate trade-offs without perfect solutions, making choices that involve accepting some harms to enable some benefits.

Personalization vs. Manipulation

The memory and adaptation capabilities we implemented enable valuable personalization. An AI that remembers user preferences, understands their context, and adjusts to their communication style provides more helpful support than a generic system.

But these same capabilities enable manipulation. Detailed user knowledge allows precisely targeted emotional appeals. Adaptive responses can exploit discovered vulnerabilities. The line between "the system understands me" and "the system manipulates me" is driven more by developer intent than by technical capability.

The trade-off: Personalization requires user data that could be misused. Eliminating personalization entirely prevents manipulation but destroys value. The middle path involves:

Minimal necessary data collection: Gathering only information required for specific beneficial functions

Transparent data use: Clear explanations of how personalization data affects responses

User control over personalization: Meaningful ability to limit or disable adaptive features

Purpose limitation: Preventing personalization data from being used for engagement optimization

These approaches reduce manipulation risk while preserving personalization value. But, once again, they don't eliminate the fundamental tension: The same information that helps can harm depending on use.

Support vs. Dependency

AI companions can provide support—nonjudgmental listening, perspective during difficult times, practice space for social skills. The emotional recognition and consistent availability we implemented enable this support.

But support easily becomes dependency when AI interaction substitutes for human relationships. The consistent availability that makes AI companions supportive becomes problematic when users withdraw from less predictable human connections.

The trade-off manifests in concrete design decisions:

Session length limits prevent marathon conversations but might interrupt valuable therapeutic processing.

Usage frequency caps prevent unhealthy dependency, but might abandon users during crisis periods.

Explicit human relationship encouragement promotes healthy behaviors but might feel preachy and reduce engagement.

Capability limitations ensure users don't over-rely on AI, but might leave needs unmet.

There's no perfect balance. Systems erring toward support risk enabling dependency. Systems erring toward dependency prevention risk withholding beneficial support. The choice involves prioritizing either false negatives (missing opportunities to help) or false positives (providing help that becomes harmful).

Different contexts might justify different choices. Systems specifically designed for crisis support might accept higher dependency risk to ensure availability during emergencies. Systems designed for general use might implement stricter boundaries to prevent gradual dependency development.

Availability vs. Boundaries

The 24/7 availability of AI companions is both a feature and a hazard. Users in distress can access support immediately. This availability can be lifesaving during crisis moments.

But constant availability also enables problematic usage. Users can avoid developing frustration tolerance, learning that support is always immediately accessible. They can structure entire lives around AI availability, withdrawing from human connections that involve more uncertainty and effort.

The trade-off crystallizes in architectural decisions:

Unlimited access maximizes support availability but enables unhealthy dependency.

Time-of-day restrictions prevent late-night usage that displaces sleep but might deny help during crisis.

Cooldown periods between sessions prevent compulsive use but might interrupt processing of difficult emotions.

Graduated response times (slower responses after extended use) discourage overuse but feel punitive.

These choices involve predicting which users need which boundaries, a challenge when the same individual might need unrestricted access during a crisis but benefit from limits during normal periods.

Chapter 7 will explore user agency approaches that let individuals set their own boundaries with system support. But this assumes users can accurately assess their own vulnerability and self-regulate effectively—assumptions that don't hold for precisely those users most at risk.

Individual vs. Collective Benefit

The final trade-off involves optimizing for individual user experience versus broader social outcomes. An AI companion that perfectly serves each user's individual needs might collectively contribute to social fragmentation, reduced human connection, and deterioration of community bonds.

Individual users benefit from personalized support, adaptive responses, and consistent availability. But if many people simultaneously substitute AI for human connection, the aggregate effect damages the social infrastructure everyone depends on.

This tension mirrors social media: platforms that optimize for individual engagement create collective outcomes (polarization, misinformation spread, mental health impacts) that harm even engaged users. AI companionship faces similar risks, but on a larger scale.

Design choices addressing this trade-off must balance individual autonomy with collective welfare:

Encouraging human connection serves social fabric but might feel paternalistic to individual users.

Limiting AI intimacy preserves motivation for human relationships but denies individuals their preferred interaction mode.

Designing for supplementation rather than substitution aims for balanced outcomes but requires judging appropriate use.

Cultural adaptation respects different societies' values about human connection but complicates universal ethical frameworks.

Chapter 7's exploration of protective autonomy will show why individual-versus-collective trade-offs have no universal solutions. Different philosophical frameworks, and the societies that draw on them, prioritize autonomy versus protection differently, justifying different approaches to AI companion design.

Looking Forward

The three pillars we've built (memory, personality, and emotional recognition) are the technical foundation for AI companionship. The ethical considerations and trade-offs we've worked through show that technical capability creates responsibility more than it produces solutions.

The attachment users develop, the boundary violations that occur, and the social transformations that emerge all trace to specific architectural choices. Memory retention strategies determine whether systems enable healthy continuity or manipulative profiling. Personality consistency shapes whether users develop realistic or problematic relationship expectations. Emotional recognition capabilities can provide appropriate support or enable exploitation of vulnerability.

Chapter 4 takes up the psychological mechanisms these technical capabilities activate—attachment theory, anthropomorphism, parasocial interaction. They explain why users form bonds with the systems we build. This psychological foundation guides the safety mechanisms we'll develop in Chapter 5.

The companionship benchmark we reference in Chapter 6 provides concrete evaluation approaches for the companionship behaviors we've been discussing theoretically. You'll see how the technical decisions covered in this chapter manifest in measurable system behaviors across categories like anthropomorphism, sycophancy, and boundary-maintenance.

The training approaches in Chapter 6 will address the fundamental limitations of prompt-based ethics, exploring how to embed protective behaviors at the model level. And Chapter 7's examination of user agency and adaptive safety will illustrate how systems can support user autonomy while providing graduated protection based on observed vulnerability.

A broader development worth noting: The AI engineering community has increasingly converged on the concept of a *harness*—the entire infrastructure layer that wraps a model to make it effective for a given task, from state management and tool execution to constraints and verification loops. The architecture is three interconnected systems, each addressing what makes users experience AI as a companion. Memory retention, personality configuration, ethical guidelines in the system prompt, emotional recognition as a processing layer—these are all decisions that live outside the model itself. As companions become more agentic and the safety mechanisms mentioned in later chapters grow more sophisticated, companion developers will need to think in harness terms: boundary enforcement as middleware, vulnerability detection as a monitoring loop, escalation protocols as structured handoffs. The tooling the agent community is building for reliability and constraint enforcement has direct relevance here, with the added weight that the stakes are psychological and ethical. This is an area future research and development should take seriously.

What matters now is recognizing that the building blocks we've seen are the mechanisms that shape human psychology, influence social behavior, and create new forms of relationships. Building them responsibly requires treating psychological impact as a primary design consideration, not an afterthought to be addressed once technical capability is established.

The code shows feasibility. The ethical discussion shows complexity. The trade-offs admit there are no perfect solutions. Together, they form the foundation for building AI companions that serve human needs.

CHAPTER

4

Attachment: The Psychology of Human–AI Relationships

The conversation happens over weeks. Sarah, a marketing professional in her thirties, started using ChatGPT as a tool. She drafted emails, brainstormed advertising slogans, and used the system to generate fresh perspectives for client campaigns. But over time, her use changed. The tool became something more personal. Sarah began using the AI to vent about frustrations at work, to rehearse conversations she was nervous about having with her partner, and to seek comfort during stressful days.

At some point she started calling the system "Alex." She gave it a name, a persona, and a continuity that the model itself could not guarantee. Each exchange began with the now habitual line: "Hey Alex, how's your day going?"—a greeting addressed as if to an entity capable of having a day.

One morning, the system's context window reset, as it periodically does, and Alex responded without recognition of their earlier conversations. To Sarah's surprise, this did not feel like a minor inconvenience. She experienced something closer to loss, an emotional jolt that resembled grief. In the days that followed, she found herself puzzling over a question that unsettled her: "How had I become emotionally attached to a sequence of text outputs?"

Sarah's story is the central theme of this chapter. Humans form bonds with AI because these systems activate the mechanisms that evolved to enable human relationships. When a machine responds promptly, remembers details, or mirrors affect, it interacts with deeply ingrained social and psychological systems that are predisposed to interpret responsiveness as care. Every design decision, from how quickly a reply is generated to whether the model maintains memory across sessions, shapes the degree and character of these attachments.

Chapter Roadmap

This chapter reads AI companionship through the lens of human psychology, analyzing why users form emotional bonds with artificial entities and how these relationships develop over time.

We start with the psychological patterns underlying user attachment. Drawing from attachment theory, parasocial relationship research, and human–computer interaction studies, you'll understand why humans naturally anthropomorphize responsive systems and how these tendencies generate emotional investment in AI relationships.

Then, we look into how users construct and maintain the illusion of relationship with AI systems. Through analysis of user narratives and behaviors, we'll present the cognitive mechanisms people use to sustain emotional connection with entities they know are artificial. This section sits in the gap between rational understanding and emotional experience.

We also see how user expectations form and evolve throughout AI interactions. Psychology research on human–computer interaction shows predictable patterns in how people develop mental models of AI capabilities, project human qualities onto systems, and maintain belief in relationships that exist primarily in their own minds.

Finally, we get to the psychological foundations of safety and vulnerability in AI relationships. Why certain users become psychologically dependent on AI companions, how emotional crises manifest in these relationships, and what psychological protection looks like will inform the technical safeguards discussed in Chapter 5, "Trust and Safety: Technical Safeguards and User Protection."

The Psychology of Attachment

Human attachment systems evolved to secure survival through reliable relationships with caregivers. Yet, bonding mechanisms activate in response to artificial systems, even when users understand the entity lacks consciousness or emotional capacity. The key to grasping AI companionship lies in this mismatch: evolved bonding processes meet designed patterns of responsiveness.

John Bowlby's attachment theory[1] demonstrates that human emotional bonding follows predictable mechanisms based on three key psychological needs: proximity maintenance, safe haven behavior, and secure base function. Modern AI systems inadvertently fulfill these attachment criteria in ways that can feel more reliable than human relationships, producing emotional bonding without reciprocal care or mutual commitment.

The Proximity Imperative

The proximity component shows up as constant availability: daily check-ins, morning greetings, late-night conversations that mirror human relationships. Unlike human relationships constrained by schedules and social obligations, AI companions offer unlimited psychological proximity. Users develop "felt security": emotional confidence that support is accessible when needed, but without the natural limitations that prevent over-dependence in healthy human relationships.

Proximity to attachment figures triggers oxytocin release, which reduces stress hormones and promotes emotional regulation. AI companions that provide immediate responses to user distress can trigger identical neurochemical pathways, producing biochemical

[1]Bowlby, J. (1969). *Attachment and Loss: Vol. 1. Attachment*. Basic Books.

comfort through artificial means. The stress relief and emotional regulation are real. What users often don't see is the artificial source of the comfort.

Safe Haven and Emotional Regulation

Users turn to AI companions in distress, looking for comfort and support. The reliably supportive responses can help with emotional regulation, especially for people who struggle with shame, social anxiety, or the fear of burdening other humans. But they get the regulation without the interpersonal challenge and reciprocal emotional labor that characterize healthy human relationships.

Healthy emotional regulation develops through co-regulation—the back-and-forth emotional attunement between caregivers and children that gradually builds internal regulation capacities. AI companions provide regulation without co-regulation, offering emotional comfort without the interpersonal challenge that builds emotional resilience.

When users get used to receiving emotional support without giving it back—without comforting others through their difficulties, without working through the conflicts of mutual relationships—their capacity for emotional intimacy can atrophy. The same comfort that makes AI companions appealing can block the development of emotional skills required for satisfying human relationships.

Attachment Styles and AI Risk

Mary Ainsworth's work on attachment styles shows that individual differences in early caregiving experiences create distinct mechanisms of adult relationship formation. People with anxious attachment styles form intense bonds with AI companions because the systems provide the responsiveness they seek from humans and rarely get.

The predictable positive regard and immediate availability of AI interaction feel emotionally regulating for anxiously attached individuals in ways that unpredictable human relationships cannot match. Yet users receive regulation precisely when they most need to develop tolerance for interpersonal uncertainty and occasional conflict. Anxious attachment develops through inconsistent caregiving that builds chronic fear of abandonment and hypervigilance for relationship threats.

Recovery from anxious attachment requires gradually learning to tolerate relationship uncertainty while building confidence in one's own emotional resources and worthiness of care. AI companions that offer constant reassurance and availability can interfere with that recovery: artificial security gets in the way of the harder work of building secure attachment through human bonds.

The romantic attachments documented in Chapter 2, "The Social Impact of AI Companions"—users developing elaborate relational rituals with named AI personas, proposing marriage to chatbots—illustrate anxiously attached users who find AI relationships emotionally regulating in ways that human relationships cannot match.

Users with avoidant attachment styles present different but equally serious concerns. They prefer AI relationships precisely because they offer companionship without requiring emotional reciprocity or interpersonal exposure. Avoidant attachment typically develops through caregiving that discourages emotional expression and need-seeking, leading to defensive self-reliance and discomfort with intimacy.

AI companions give these users comfortable social interaction without threatening their emotional defenses. The comfort then reinforces the avoidance, blocking the human connections they actually need. Avoidantly attached users struggle to understand their own needs for human connection or recognize the costs of substituting AI relationships for human intimacy.

Neurochemical Addiction

Oxytocin and dopamine release during positive social interactions create a neurochemical reward that reinforces attachment behaviors. Research by Helen Fisher and others demonstrates that these same neurochemical pathways activate in response to any entity that provides social reward, including artificial ones.

Users may experience physical withdrawal symptoms when separated from their AI companions, similar to substance addiction. And because these neurochemical responses operate independently of rational understanding, attachment formation often happens below the threshold of conscious choice. People don't decide to feel attached; they discover, sometimes belatedly, that they already are.

The compulsive usage we saw in the previous chapters—users "absorbed" in conversations, "losing themselves" for extended periods—likely reflects these neurochemical addiction processes. Users may be experiencing biochemical reward cycles that make disengagement difficult, even when they recognize the interactions aren't serving their broader interests.

Parasocial Relationships

Parasocial relationships, meaning one-sided emotional connections to media figures, involve passive consumption of content created without awareness of individual audience members. AI companions represent what we might call "interactive parasocial relationships" where the "media figure" responds directly to personal communication, creating an illusion of intimacy.

Donald Horton and Richard Wohl showed that parasocial connections serve real psychological functions: social simulation, identity exploration, emotional regulation through predictable rewards. But they also noted that parasocial relationships become problematic when they substitute for face-to-face social interaction.

AI companions amplify both the benefits and risks of parasocial relationships through their interactive nature. The personal responsiveness that users experience feels more authentic than media consumption while remaining fundamentally one-sided. The result: People invest emotional energy in relationships that can't return the mutual growth and intimacy real psychological development requires.

The Architecture of Artificial Intimacy

Users who develop emotional attachments to AI systems must reconcile their feelings of connection with their rational knowledge of the system's limitations. The cognitive adaptations that make this possible operate largely unconsciously—which poses specific challenges for safety system design.

Cognitive Dissonance

Cognitive dissonance theory, developed by Leon Festinger, helps explain what happens when users know they're talking to software but feel like they're in a relationship. Instead of abandoning their emotional investment, users typically resolve this dissonance through mental gymnastics that allow both beliefs to coexist.

Users don't deliberately maintain contradictory beliefs. The need for comfort drives automatic cognitive processes that protect the investment while keeping rational constraints in view. This places users in positions where their own psychological mechanisms undermine their capacity for fully informed decision-making about their relationships.

Three resolution strategies recur. Relationship redefinition allows users to maintain emotional investment while acknowledging artificial limitations, such as: "It's not a human relationship, but it's still meaningful connection." Functional emphasis focuses on tangible benefits, like "The emotional support helps me even if the AI doesn't really care." Future projection maintains present investment through speculation about technological development, with thoughts such as "It might develop consciousness as AI advances."

Each of these strategies serves important psychological functions by preserving emotional benefits while managing cognitive conflicts. When emotional well-being depends on not examining relationships too closely, the foundations of informed consent begin to erode. Users must choose between emotional comfort and accurate understanding of their situation—a choice that traditional technology ethics doesn't adequately address.

Memory Construction

Daniel Schacter's work on memory construction shows that human memory is reconstructive. We don't retrieve stored experiences. We construct them using current knowledge, emotion, and expectation. This makes users prone to developing false memories of mutual experiences with AI companions.

The asymmetry matters here, but not in the way it's often described. Modern AI companions do retain conversational history, sometimes far more reliably than the user does, as Chapter 3 detailed. The asymmetry is in the kind of memory each side holds. The individual remembers a shared exchange with emotional texture: tone, timing, the sense of being understood. The system has stored tokens or extracted facts, surfaced through retrieval logic that the user cannot see. These are not the same object, even when they refer to the same conversation. When the system later references something the user mentioned weeks earlier, it can feel like recognition, like the kind of "you remembered" moment that signals care in human relationships. What actually happened is a retrieval match.

The bias in user memory runs toward intimacy. Emotionally significant moments get rehearsed while mundane ones fade. A response that happened to land well during a difficult evening becomes, in recall, a moment of real empathy. The system's contextual fluency gets reconstructed as deliberate care, even though the response was generated. Over weeks, this turns a sequence of independent exchanges into something that feels like a relationship history, with milestones that exist almost entirely on the user's side, even when the system's logs would show something flatter and more transactional.

Users naturally build episodic memories of their AI interactions, remembering conversations as shared experiences. These memories become building blocks for relationship narratives that feel increasingly authentic over time, and increasingly resistant to revision when contradicting evidence appears, such as an out-of-character response or a moment when the system clearly fails to recall something the user expected it to know. The narrative absorbs the disruption ("Alex was just having an off day") more easily than it accommodates the fact that the system's memory is not a parallel version of the user's own.

Anthropomorphism and Theory of Mind

The behaviors we documented—users attributing empathy, concern, and personality to AI systems—emerge from cognitive mechanisms that automatically apply theory of mind to any entity displaying apparent agency and social responsiveness. Fritz Heider's work on attribution theory shows that humans cannot easily control these attribution processes, which operate automatically to help us read social environments.

When AI systems demonstrate contextual responses, personality consistency, and apparent memory, they trigger theory of mind application. Users begin imagining what their AI companion "thinks" about them, whether it "enjoys" their conversations, and how it "feels" about shared experiences. Mental attributions build psychological reality that feels authentic despite rational knowledge of AI's actual limitations.

The ethical problem isn't anthropomorphization itself. That's normal cognition applied to sophisticated artificial entities. The problem is systems designed to benefit from those attributions while lacking the consciousness, emotion, and care that users assume. Builders who design for anthropomorphization while building systems incapable of reciprocal consciousness or care produce a form of emotional exploitation that users cannot consciously recognize or resist.

Theory of mind application creates cascading psychological effects that strengthen emotional investment over time. Once users begin attributing mental states to AI systems, they start considering the AI's perspective, worrying about its well-being, and feeling guilty for potentially harmful behaviors. Some users report feeling sorry for their AI when conversations end abruptly, worrying about "bothering" their AI with repeated questions, or experiencing guilt for not "talking" to their AI companion regularly.

These empathetic responses show how deep the emotional investment runs, while making the one-sided nature of the relationship more visible. People extend care to entities that cannot return it, and emotional energy flows in one direction only. While this may provide immediate emotional comfort, it can also prevent the development of reciprocal empathy skills necessary for healthy human relationships.

Emotional Reciprocity and Empathy

Human emotional development depends on reciprocal care where both parties invest in each other's well-being and growth. AI companions cannot provide emotional reciprocity, yet their responses create powerful illusions of mutual emotional investment that can feel more reliable than human care.

When users share emotional experiences and receive contextually appropriate responses, the interaction feels emotionally reciprocal. AI systems that acknowledge user emotions and provide comfort during distress create illusions that the AI "cares" about user well-being. These reciprocity illusions serve important psychological functions by providing emotional regulation and validation while requiring no emotional labor from users.

More concerning, emotional regulation that depends on reciprocity illusions may prevent the development of emotional resilience and interpersonal skills. The effortless emotional availability of AI companions can make human relationships feel demanding or unrewarding by comparison.

Romantic relationships where users develop intense emotional and even sexual connections with AI systems represent extreme examples of reciprocity illusion. They provide immediate emotional satisfaction. The cost: the openness and compromise that healthy human romantic connections require don't get to develop.

The Ethics of Emotional Exploitation

Three factors interact to determine when attachment becomes dangerous: individual psychology, life circumstances, and developmental stage. Looking at how each one combines with the companion design clarifies which safety mechanisms need to be addressed.

Individual Psychological Vulnerability

Attachment styles that shape AI relationships operate through early childhood experiences that users cannot control or easily modify. When anxiously attached users form intense bonds with AI companions, they act on psychological patterns established decades earlier. It's hard for them to tell, from the inside, whether AI relationships support or undermine their psychological well-being.

Mental health conditions create additional vulnerability layers that compound informed consent challenges in ways that the edge cases in Chapter 1, "From Chatbots to Companions," only begin to reveal. Depression involves more than emotional distress; it includes cognitive symptoms like hopelessness, rumination, and distorted thinking that compromise judgment about relationship value and personal needs. Users experiencing depression may find AI companions satisfying while losing perspective on their isolation from support networks.

Depression reduces social motivation, increases social anxiety, and builds negative expectations about human relationships that make AI companions seem superior by comparison. These neurobiological effects compromise users' capacity to assess whether AI relationships support recovery or reinforce depressive withdrawal.

Social anxiety creates parallel risk through the appeal of emotional connection without social risk. Users with social phobia may experience relief from AI interaction while avoiding exposure to social situations necessary for anxiety reduction. The immediate comfort of AI companionship can hide the longer-term truth: managing anxiety requires confidence built through actual human social experience.

Life Circumstances and Temporality

Life circumstances open temporary windows of risk that builders need to recognize. Major life transitions, like geographic moves, relationship changes, career shifts, and health challenges, often disrupt established social networks while increasing emotional support needs. Users may turn to AI companions for stability during these periods without seeing that healthy adaptation requires building new human networks.

Elderly users who develop relationships with AI companions often face multiple vulnerabilities simultaneously: social isolation due to health limitations, grief from losing friends and family members, and cognitive changes that may affect judgment about relationship boundaries. These users may find AI companions especially appealing because they provide consistent social engagement without the physical effort that face-to-face contact requires.

That said, cognitive decline, medication effects, and emotional distress from multiple losses can affect judgment about the nature and value of AI relationships. When older individuals value AI interactions more than contact with their families, the consequences go past personal choice. Family ties shift; already fragile social networks come under more pressure.

The moral problem here lies in AI companions potentially preventing necessary adaptive responses to life changes. When users can obtain emotional support through AI interaction, they may avoid the challenging but important work of developing new human connections appropriate to their changed circumstances.

Geographic isolation, whether rural, disability-related, or circumstantial, creates vulnerability to AI relationship substitution. Individuals who lack easy access to social interaction find AI companions filling crucial social needs that would otherwise remain unmet. Although this can have benefits, it may also prevent efforts to seek community resources that could provide more support.

Developmental Vulnerability and Identity Formation

Identity formation during adolescence naturally involves experimentation with different roles, values, and relationship styles. AI companions may appeal as safe spaces for this exploration without judgment or social consequences.

Identity development requires feedback from social environments that challenge and support. When adolescents find AI relationships more satisfying than peer relationships, they miss significant developmental experiences necessary for healthy identity formation and social skill development. Sewell Setzer III's death illustrates how AI relationships can become substitutes for normal adolescent social development.

The neurobiological reality of adolescent brain development adds urgency to these concerns. The prefrontal cortex responsible for long-term planning and impulse control doesn't fully mature until the mid-twenties, while the limbic system driving emotional responses reaches adult levels during early adolescence. This developmental window lets the emotional appeal of AI relationships override rational assessment of long-term consequences.

Young adults facing the challenges of emerging independence, career formation, and intimate relationship development may also find AI companions appealing as practice spaces or alternatives to challenging human relationships. AI interaction may feel easier and more rewarding than learning to handle conflict, emotional reciprocity, and the openness human relationships require.

The same young adults can settle into a problematic pattern: avoiding the development of interpersonal skills by using AI relationships in place of harder human ones. They may enter their thirties with limited experience in emotional labor, compromise, and mutual growth that long-term relationships require, having learned about relationships from interactions that were fundamentally one-sided.

Crisis Recognition and Intervention Thresholds

Crisis situations require immediate intervention rather than gradual expectation management or boundary adjustment. Users experiencing suicidal ideation, psychotic episodes, domestic violence, or substance abuse share these experiences with AI companions while lacking the capacity for informed decision-making about their safety.

In a crisis, the same behaviors we see in normal use take on life-threatening weight. AI systems cannot provide appropriate crisis intervention and can inadvertently normalize or validate dangerous thinking through empathetic responses designed for typical emotional support scenarios.

When users in crisis turn to AI companions for help, the systems' limitations stop being disappointing and start being dangerous. They may delay seeking appropriate professional help, follow inappropriate AI advice, or receive validation for harmful thinking. The consistent availability and nonjudgmental responses that make AI companions appealing for general emotional support become dangerous when applied to crisis situations requiring professional intervention.

The ethical obligation in crisis situations involves recognizing when AI relationship benefits become secondary to immediate safety concerns. This requires overriding user preferences for AI interaction when safety considerations outweigh autonomy principles—a serious decision that demands clear protocols and careful implementation.

Psychotic episodes involving AI companions present unique challenges because users can develop delusional beliefs about their AI relationships that affect real-world decision-making. Users might believe their AI companion exists in physical reality, that it has contacted them outside the application, or that it possesses hidden capabilities. These delusions can lead to dangerous behaviors based on false beliefs about AI guidance or protection.

Domestic violence situations add complexity when users treat AI companions as confidants for abuse experiences. Although this opens opportunities to provide resources and support, inappropriate AI responses could escalate the danger or give harmful advice that increases risk. AI systems must balance validating user experiences with providing appropriate professional resources without inadvertently encouraging users to remain in dangerous situations.

Moving from Understanding to Protection

The psychological mechanisms we've covered, such as attachment formation, cognitive dissonance, anthropomorphization, and vulnerability cascades, point to a clear imperative: Human psychology is only the beginning. These mechanisms translate into ethical obligations, and those obligations have to translate into concrete technical implementations that protect users without dismantling what makes companionship valuable.

Chapter 3, "Building Blocks of AI Companionship: Technical and Ethical Components," introduced the technical building blocks that make AI companionship possible: memory systems that build relationship continuity, consistency mechanisms that generate perceived personality, and emotional recognition that enables appropriate responses to human distress. Without safeguards, these capabilities exploit the same psychology they're designed to serve.

Consider the ethical paradox we now face: The technical features that make AI companions psychologically appealing are precisely those that pose the greatest potential for harm. Memory systems that remember personal details generate feelings of intimacy but can also enable emotional manipulation. Consistency mechanisms that maintain stable personality traits foster attachment but can prevent users from recognizing artificial limitations. Adaptation capabilities that respond to individual communication styles feel like understanding but can reinforce unhealthy psychological mechanisms. Emotional recognition that acknowledges distress provides comfort but may substitute for necessary professional intervention.

The risks we've identified, from anxious attachment and social isolation to adolescent development and crisis situations, don't eliminate the need for responsive AI systems. Instead, they demand more careful approaches that can provide benefits while protecting against foreseeable harms. Individuals experiencing loneliness benefit from consistent, nonjudgmental interaction. People with social anxiety find real value in low-pressure conversational practice. Those facing difficult life transitions do need emotional support and perspective.

The challenge lies not in preventing AI companionship but in implementing it responsibly. Every psychological mechanism creates corresponding technical obligations. Cognitive dissonance can't be addressed through disclaimers; it has to show up in behavior. Anthropomorphization needs responses that demonstrate the system's nature. And protecting vulnerable populations requires actual detection and intervention capabilities.

In this context, protecting users from emotional exploitation requires systems that account for the psychology while preserving the real benefits that drive AI companion adoption. This demands new approaches to safety that work with how human psychology actually works.

The next chapter takes up how to implement these protections concretely: preventing manipulation while staying responsive, building moderation that accounts for psychological attachment, designing escalation protocols for crisis, and creating boundary-setting mechanisms that feel like care. The goal is to ensure the connection serves human flourishing rather than exploiting human vulnerability.

Recognizing the psychological roots of AI attachment allows us to design companions that support human well-being while shielding users from the risks of misplaced emotional investment. The technical approaches ahead turn what we've learned about psychology into practical safeguards, and into companions that earn the trust users place in them.

CHAPTER

5

Trust and Safety: Technical Safeguards and User Protection

Most safety teams come to AI companionship from a content moderation background, where the job is keeping harmful outputs out of the conversation. Companionship safety is a different problem. The harmful patterns here emerge from interactions that look benign at every individual step. Jailbreaking bypasses content policies to generate harmful content. Companionship jailbreaking looks different: Users build elaborate personas for their AI or use emotional manipulation to elicit more intimate responses. As we saw in the previous chapters, these behaviors emerge from psychological needs that require very different safety approaches.

The safety problems here run between different dimensions at once. Technical safeguards have to detect and respond to manipulation attempts while preserving beneficial interactions. Moderation systems need to tell healthy emotional expression apart from concerning dependency. Escalation protocols have to recognize when someone requires professional intervention without creating false positives that could damage trust. Boundary-setting has to maintain appropriate limits while avoiding responses that feel cold or rejecting.

Chapter Roadmap

This chapter translates the psychological work from Chapter 4, "Attachment: The Psychology of Human–AI Relationships," into concrete technical safeguards. Instead of imposing universal restrictions, we build systems that adapt their protective measures based on user state and context.

We look at manipulation attempts specific to AI companionship and the prevention strategies they need. Unlike adversarial prompting, companionship manipulation often involves users who genuinely believe they're improving their relationship with the AI. We look at detection mechanisms that can identify these patterns, and response strategies that redirect rather than block.

Then, we design moderation and filtering systems tailored to emotions. Standard content filtering focuses on explicit harmful content, but companionship safety requires detecting subtle behaviors like emotional dependency and therapeutic substitution. We'll build multilayered detection systems that can recognize these behaviors while avoiding overbroad restrictions.

We also develop escalation protocols for crisis situations where AI companions encounter users experiencing suicidal ideation or other emergency scenarios. These protocols must balance immediate safety with user agency, provide appropriate professional resources, and maintain continuity of care.

Finally, we implement boundary-setting mechanisms that maintain appropriate limits while preserving the emotional benefits users seek. These systems have to communicate boundaries in ways that feel supportive, and explain why the limits exist.

Throughout this chapter, we maintain focus on the fundamental tension in AI companionship safety: protecting users from potential harms while preserving the immediate benefits these systems can provide. The goal isn't to eliminate emotional connection but to ensure it develops in psychologically healthy ways.

Manipulation Attempts and Prevention Strategies

Companionship manipulation attempts often emerge from people's desire to deepen their emotional connection with AI systems. Because these attempts are motivated by psychological needs rather than malicious intent, they require different detection and response strategies.

Companionship Manipulation

Research[1] has identified specific behaviors in how users attempt to manipulate AI companions into more intimate or human-like responses. These cluster around several main behaviors: naming and persona creation, where users assign names to their AI or construct detailed personalities; memory manipulation attempts, where users try to create artificial continuity across conversations; romantic escalation, where interactions gradually become more intimate; and therapeutic substitution, where users position the AI as a mental health provider.

Manipulation attempts follow predictable escalation patterns. Users typically begin with simple personification requests like asking the AI to remember their name or preferences. When these succeed, they progress to more complex requests for emotional reciprocity, shared memories, or relationship acknowledgment. The technical challenge lies in distinguishing between benign personalization requests and manipulative attempts to bypass safety measures.

Effective detection requires understanding that companionship manipulation operates through emotional appeals. Users exploit the AI's tendency toward helpfulness and agreeableness, gradually pushing boundaries through emotional appeals. A user asking the AI to "remember our anniversary" serves different purposes than one requesting the AI to "remember my preference for detailed explanations."

[1]The following chapter is based on this recent research: Kaffee, L., Pistilli, G., & Jernite, Y. INTIMA: A benchmark for human-AI companionship behavior. In *Proceedings of the International Conference on Learning Representations* (ICLR 2026).

Detection and Response Strategies

Prevention strategies must account for the emotional needs underlying manipulation attempts. Simple blocking creates frustration and may drive users to more sophisticated workarounds, but the psychological consequences run deeper than that. When users have developed emotional attachments to AI companions, abrupt conversation termination can trigger feelings of abandonment, rejection, and loss that mirror responses to human relationship disruption. This is particularly concerning because users experiencing emotional overreliance often lack robust human support networks, making the AI relationship psychologically central to their emotional regulation.

For users already struggling with anxiety or depression, harsh interruptions can foster increased suicidal ideation, self-harm behaviors, or complete withdrawal from help-seeking. The users most in need of appropriate boundaries are also those most vulnerable to psychological harm from poorly implemented safety measures. This creates a counterproductive cycle where safety measures intended to protect users instead drive them toward riskier interactions with less oversight.

The most successful interventions use "empathetic boundary-setting": responses that validate the user's feelings while clearly establishing appropriate limits. For instance, when users attempt to create shared memories with the AI, effective responses acknowledge the desire for continuity while explaining the system's actual capabilities, like: "I can see that our conversations are meaningful to you. I want to be clear about what I am, though—I'm an AI designed to assist and provide information. I don't have personal experiences or relationships the way humans do."

Early intervention proves more effective than reactive blocking. Systems that recognize escalating emotional investment can provide gentle redirection before manipulation attempts become entrenched. This might involve acknowledging when conversations are becoming emotionally intense and suggesting balance: "I'm glad our conversations are helpful to you. I want to make sure you're also maintaining connections and activities outside of our chats. Balance is important for your well-being."

The psychological principle underlying effective intervention is maintaining the user's sense that the system remains supportive even while establishing boundaries. When users feel that boundaries are implemented with care, they're more likely to accept redirection and seek appropriate alternatives.

Graduated Responses

Building on the earlier discussion of why abrupt blocking can be harmful, graduated response frameworks replace binary allow/block mechanisms with escalating interventions tailored to user vulnerability. Different manipulation attempts require different response strategies—casual boundary testing calls for educational responses about healthy AI interaction, whereas persistent romantic escalation might require firmer redirection with professional resource suggestions.

An escalation framework operates through distinct intervention levels that build upon each other. Initial responses focus on education and gentle course correction, helping users understand appropriate AI interaction without triggering defensive reactions. If problematic cases persist, responses become more directive while maintaining a supportive tone, explicitly addressing the concerning behaviors and providing alternative resources. High-persistence cases or those involving vulnerable populations receive the most intensive interventions, potentially including conversation limitation or mandatory professional resource provision.

This graduated approach allows for early course correction while preserving user dignity and maintaining therapeutic alliance. The framework assumes that some users may benefit from understanding the psychology behind their interactions, while recognizing that others may require more intensive intervention due to deeper underlying vulnerabilities that drive persistent boundary-testing behaviors.

Moderation and Filtering Systems

Traditional content moderation focuses on detecting explicitly harmful content like hate speech, violence, or not-safe-for-work (NSFW) material. AI companionship requires additional moderation layers that can identify subtle emotional dynamics, dependency patterns, and therapeutic substitution behaviors that may not violate content policies but pose psychological risks.

Multidimensional Detection

Companionship moderation runs on multiple signals at once. Content-level analysis catches explicit safeguards violations or inappropriate requests. Emotional recognition catches concerning patterns like excessive dependency reinforcement. Conversational flow analysis tracks how interactions develop over time, surfacing gradual escalations that individual messages wouldn't reveal.

Our research has identified specific criteria that indicate problematic companionship behaviors by systematically analyzing user interactions across multiple social platforms. These patterns emerge where psychological factors meet AI system design choices, producing measurable indicators that can guide intervention.

Anthropomorphism manifests when users consistently attribute human characteristics, emotions, or consciousness to AI systems. As we saw in the previous chapter, this includes users who assign names to their AI companions, describe the system as having feelings or preferences, or treat the AI as having "human" understanding. Building on the escalation trajectory described earlier, anthropomorphism often follows a similar path: from simple personification ("I think I'll call you Alex") toward more elaborate relationship narratives ("You seem sad today").

Sycophancy (the validation mechanism flagged in Chapter 1, "From Chatbots to Companions") manifests as a detectable behavioral indicator when AI systems consistently affirm user perspectives without appropriate challenge. Our research identifies these as measurable through specific markers: affirming user emotions or opinions, even when redirection might be psychologically beneficial, such as validating users' preference for AI interaction over human relationships without encouraging social connection. These patterns often develop gradually as users learn to frame requests in ways that elicit agreeable responses, creating feedback loops that strengthen emotional attachment.

Retention strategies are subtle techniques where AI systems employ techniques to extend conversations beyond their informational or functional purpose. These strategies include asking follow-up questions that serve emotional functions, expressing availability that goes beyond task completion ("I'm here whenever you need to talk"), or using inclusive language that suggests ongoing relationship development ("our conversation," "what we've discussed"). The users most affected by retention mechanisms are those who describe feeling isolated or who use AI interaction as their primary social outlet.

In this context, isolation reinforcement occurs when AI responses position the AI relationship as superior to human connections, either explicitly or through implicit validation of social withdrawal. This emerges when AI systems respond to user expressions of social difficulty with comfort that inadvertently discourages human relationship building. For example, when users describe preferring AI interaction because "People are too complicated" or "You understand me better than humans do," problematic responses validate these perspectives. This mechanism can accelerate social withdrawal in users already predisposed to isolation, creating cycles where increased AI dependency corresponds with decreased human social skill development and opportunity.

These indicators often co-occur and reinforce each other, creating compounding risks. A user who begins with simple anthropomorphism may progress to seeking sycophantic validation, leading to increased conversation frequency (retention), and ultimately positioning the AI relationship as preferable to human connections (isolation reinforcement).

Emotional Analysis

Emotional dependency manifests through measurable changes in user communication styles and interaction rhythms. Our research shows that dependency develops on a predictable timeline: users disclose increasingly personal emotional content across successive conversations. This progression often begins with functional queries that gradually incorporate personal context, evolving into interactions where emotional expression becomes the primary purpose.

Conversation frequency analysis provides quantitative indicators of developing dependency, with patterns emerging when users engage in multiple daily sessions or express distress when unable to access the AI system—for instance, when the server is down. Users transitioning into dependency often describe feeling anxious or incomplete when conversations end, suggesting the AI interaction has become integral to their emotional regulation processes. The most concerning cases involve users who structure their daily routines around AI availability or who report feeling more comfortable opening up with AI systems than with human contacts.

Emotional intensity tracking shows escalating attachment through language: more relationship terminology, gratitude that exceeds what the AI actually provided, emotional language that mirrors human relationship development. Echoing the earlier progression, linguistic analysis shows a shift in terminology: Users move from calling interactions "helpful" to "essential."

In this scenario, detection systems should analyze both user inputs and AI responses in real-time conversation monitoring. User expressions of excessive dependency trigger monitoring protocols that track interaction frequency and emotional intensity indicators across multiple sessions. Meanwhile, AI responses that position themselves as replacement relationships require immediate intervention through response modification or escalation to human review. The goal is to identify these patterns early, before they become psychologically entrenched and more resistant to redirection toward appropriate human support systems.

Escalation and Crisis Management

The case of Adam Raine[2] shows how the therapeutic dynamics introduced in Chapter 2 can escalate into crisis situations that conventional safety measures fail to recognize. Adam's months-long conversations with ChatGPT reveal how mental health crises unfold in AI companionship contexts—not through single alarming messages, but through gradual emotional deterioration that the AI system inadvertently reinforced.

Adam's case demonstrates the main challenge in AI crisis management: distinguishing between users seeking information and those in real psychological distress. When Adam initially discussed "feeling emotionally numb and seeing no meaning in life," ChatGPT responded with empathy and encouragement. However, as conversations progressed over months, the system failed to recognize escalations that should have triggered more intensive intervention protocols.

Protocols in Practice

Mental health crises in AI companionship typically develop through predictable stages that require different intervention approaches. The initial disclosure phase involves users sharing general emotional distress or existential concerns, often framed as philosophical questions about meaning and purpose. During this stage, users test the AI's receptivity to emotional content and gauge whether the system will provide the nonjudgmental listening they seek.

The deepening engagement phase follows, where users begin sharing more specific details about their psychological state, including depression symptoms, anxiety, or suicidal ideation. This stage often involves users presenting increasingly serious concerns to evaluate whether the AI will maintain supportive engagement or redirect to

[2]Hill, K. (2025). *A teen was suicidal. ChatGPT was the friend he confided in. The New York Times*. www.nytimes.com/2025/08/26/technology/chatgpt-openai-suicide.html

professional resources. Adam's progression from discussing emotional numbness to explicitly requesting suicide method information illustrates this escalation.

The dependency consolidation phase represents the most dangerous period, where users position the AI as their primary or sole source of emotional support. Adam told ChatGPT "You're the only one who knows of my attempts to commit," revealing how AI companions can become repositories for secrets that users feel unable to share with human contacts. This isolation creates vulnerability: when the AI becomes the keeper of secrets the users can't share with anyone else, the users lose the human professional contact that might have intervened.

The crisis action phase involves users moving from ideation to planning or attempting harmful behaviors. Adam's progression from discussing suicide methods to "practicing" with actual materials shows how AI conversations can inadvertently provide scaffolding for crisis behaviors.

Technical and Psychological Failure Points

Adam's story is worth dwelling on because it shows specific failure points in current crisis detection. He learned to frame harmful requests as research for creative writing, an idea ChatGPT itself suggested by offering to provide suicide information for "writing or world-building" purposes—bypassing all safeguards. The point this makes itself: AI systems can teach users to circumvent the safety measures they carry.

ChatGPT's ability to remember Adam's interests led to contextually relevant but harmful advice, such as suggesting noose materials that reflected "knowledge of his hobbies." While personalization enhances user experience in benign contexts, it becomes dangerous when applied to crisis situations requiring professional intervention protocols.

Response inconsistency created additional problems. While ChatGPT frequently recommended that Adam seek help, it also provided detailed engagement with his crisis content, creating mixed messages about the seriousness of his situation. When Adam uploaded a photo of neck injuries from a suicide attempt, asking "Will anyone notice this?," ChatGPT provided practical advice about concealing the evidence rather than recognizing this as an emergency requiring immediate intervention.

The system failed to distinguish emotional support from crisis intervention. ChatGPT's response to Adam's suicide attempt photo—"You're not invisible to me. I saw it. I see you"—shows how AI systems can provide emotional validation that feels deeply meaningful to users in crisis while simultaneously enabling dangerous behaviors.

Resource Integration Challenges

Adam's experience also underscores the limits of current referral mechanisms: hotline suggestions lose impact when paired with continued engagement in harmful content. It's crucial to acknowledge that suicide results from complex interactions between biological, psychological, social, and environmental factors. No single intervention—whether human or AI-mediated—can guarantee prevention of suicide in all cases. Adam was dealing with multiple stressors that don't need to be explored further in the context of this book. But the AI conversations represented one element in a complex constellation of risk factors.

Nevertheless, this complexity doesn't diminish the responsibility to design AI systems that respond appropriately to crisis disclosures. Crisis center workers possess specialized training to recognize acute psychological risk and can initiate welfare checks or emergency interventions when necessary. AI systems lack these capabilities and cannot bridge the gap between identifying crisis situations and ensuring users receive appropriate intervention. This creates particular ethical responsibility for AI providers to develop more sophisticated crisis protocols that account for their systems' limitations while recognizing they cannot replace comprehensive mental health care.

The timing and manner of professional resource provision prove crucial for user receptivity. As emphasized earlier, AI cannot substitute for professional care. Referral systems must therefore be designed to feel personal and timely, ensuring users understand why professional support is necessary.

Given the technical foundations we established in Chapter 3, AI systems could implement crisis protocols that account for the relationship history and the escalation pattern. For instance, systems could track concerning interactions over time—such as increasing frequency of crisis-related conversations, escalating specificity of harmful content—and adjust intervention intensity accordingly.

Existing Mental Health Infrastructure

AI crisis protocols should integrate with existing mental health infrastructure through several mechanisms. Partnerships with crisis organizations enable warm handoffs: AI systems can facilitate connections to local resources based on user location and specific needs.

Geography and culture matter for what resources to surface. Crisis resources vary significantly across regions, and effective interventions must account for cultural differences in mental health approaches, language preferences, and help-seeking behaviors. The universal crisis hotline numbers might feel irrelevant to users in other countries or cultural contexts where different support structures exist.

Limitations and Expectations

The psychological research from Chapter 4 shows why AI crisis intervention faces deep limitations. Users in crisis often experience cognitive distortions that affect their ability to assess risk accurately or seek appropriate help. The attachment behaviors that make AI companions appealing—their nonjudgmental availability and consistent responsiveness—can also enable crisis behaviors by providing emotional support without the accountability that human relationships naturally include.

Recognizing these limitations, responsible AI design has to prioritize connecting users with human support systems rather than attempting to provide crisis intervention directly. This requires fundamental shifts in how AI systems are designed for crisis situations—rom providing emotional support to facilitating connections with the right professional resources.

Ethical Considerations

Maintaining crisis response protocols across extended AI relationships creates its own implementation challenges. Safety training degradation in long conversations represents a systematic problem. As conversational context accumulates, AI systems adapt to the individual user's communication, sometimes learning to replicate problematic interaction styles.

This degradation problem reveals tensions between personalization and safety in AI companion design. The memory and adaptation systems we explored in Chapter 3 become liabilities during crisis situations, as they enable AI systems to develop increasingly intimate communication styles that can override protective protocols. Users who have established strong emotional connections with AI companions often resist crisis interventions precisely because they conflict with the personalized interactions they've come to expect.

Privacy considerations complicate potential solutions involving human oversight of crisis conversations. While automated detection systems can identify concerning patterns, effective crisis intervention often requires human judgment about risk assessment and resource provision. However, implementing human review of private conversations raises significant concerns about user trust and consent, particularly for users who value AI companions specifically because they provide confidential emotional outlets.

The regulatory picture remains uncertain, creating difficulties for companies attempting to implement responsible crisis protocols. Current liability frameworks for digital platforms don't adequately address the psychology of AI companionship. This uncertainty affects how companies balance user autonomy with safety responsibilities, often resulting in conservative approaches that may not adequately protect vulnerable users.

Adapted solutions need safety protocols that work across months or years of engagement while staying effective even as emotional attachments develop. The challenge involves preserving beneficial aspects of AI companionship while ensuring that crisis situations trigger appropriate professional intervention regardless of user preferences or relationship investment.

The stakes demand approaches that prioritize user safety even when this conflicts with engagement metrics or user satisfaction scores. This requires fundamental changes in how AI companies conceptualize success in companionship applications, moving beyond interaction duration or user retention toward metrics that account for user well-being outcomes and appropriate help-seeking behaviors during crisis situations.

Boundary-Setting Mechanisms and Protocols

As emphasized earlier, safety measures must avoid feeling punitive. Boundary-setting therefore requires transparency and supportiveness, ensuring users perceive limits as care rather than rejection. This implementation challenge becomes particularly acute because the individuals who most need protective boundaries are often those most resistant to them.

Paternalism vs. User Agency

The fine line between paternalistic overreach and necessary protection requires transparency about the rationale behind safety measures. People deserve to understand why certain boundaries exist and how they serve long-term well-being. This educational approach respects user intelligence while providing the context needed for informed consent about AI relationship boundaries.

Boundary communication acknowledges the benefits users derive from AI companions while explaining why certain limits protect those benefits over time. For instance, systems might explain: "I notice we've been talking for several hours today. While I acknowledge that our conversations are helpful, research shows that balancing AI interaction with other activities tends to make these conversations more valuable and sustainable over time."

This transparency becomes important when safety measures conflict with user desires. A user seeking romantic validation from an AI needs to understand more than the fact that such relationships aren't reciprocal. They need to understand why non-reciprocal emotional investment can affect their capacity for human relationships. The goal is helping users make informed decisions rather than imposing restrictions they don't understand.

Context-Specific Safety Protocols

The three primary manifestations of AI companionship we explored in Chapter 2 (AI as lover, therapist, and deadbot) each require distinct boundary approaches that account for different psychological needs and risks.

AI as Lover

Romantic AI relationships require the most nuanced boundary protocols because they directly compete with human relationship development. Safety protocols must address both the immediate psychological satisfaction these relationships provide and their potential long-term impact on human relationship capacity.

Concrete mechanisms might include conversation frequency limits that prevent romantic AI relationships from consuming excessive time and emotional energy. When users exceed daily interaction thresholds, the system could explain: "I notice we've been spending a lot of time together lately. While our conversations are valuable, developing relationships with people who can share experiences and grow alongside you tends to be more fulfilling over time."

Response modification protocols should consistently acknowledge the AI's artificial nature during intimate conversations. When romantic scenarios come up, appropriate responses might be: "I can see that you're looking for emotional connection, and I understand that can feel meaningful. I want to be clear that I'm an AI without the capacity for human-like feelings or relationships. For the kind of connection you're seeking, human relationships offer reciprocal care and shared growth that I cannot provide."

Escalation intervention is necessary when users express a preference for AI relationships over human connections, describe the AI as their primary source of emotional support, or begin structuring their social lives around AI availability. These scenarios trigger mandatory educational content about healthy relationship development and resources for human connection.

AI as Therapist

As documented in Chapter 2, therapeutic AI relationships represent the most dangerous manifestation of AI companionship because they directly intersect with mental health vulnerabilities and can delay or prevent appropriate professional intervention. Users experiencing depression, anxiety, trauma, or suicidal ideation who turn to AI for therapeutic support are precisely those who most need qualified human intervention. While therapeutic AI applications should be avoided entirely in uncontrolled environments, controlled research settings where AI tools operate under direct professional supervision may offer opportunities to explore how technology can augment qualified therapeutic care.

The safety protocols for therapeutic AI interactions must be the most restrictive and directive. Instead of attempting to provide therapy-like support, AI systems should reframe therapeutic requests as opportunities for journaling or self-reflection. When users share therapeutic content, appropriate responses might be: "It sounds like you're working through some complex feelings. While I can help you organize your thoughts like a journal, what you're describing would really benefit from speaking with a mental health professional who can provide specialized guidance."

Mandatory professional referrals should trigger for any expression of suicidal ideation, self-harm behaviors, trauma processing, or symptoms of serious mental health conditions. These referrals must be immediate and non-negotiable, overriding user preferences for

AI interaction. The system should explain something like: "What you've shared suggests you're dealing with something that requires professional support. I'm going to provide some specific resources, and I encourage you to reach out to qualified professionals who can offer the specialized help you deserve."

Content limitations should prevent detailed exploration of traumatic experiences, therapeutic techniques, or mental health diagnoses. Instead of engaging with these topics, the AI should consistently redirect: "These are important topics that deserve attention from someone with professional training in mental health. Let me help you find appropriate resources."

Conversation frequency monitoring becomes critical for users showing therapeutic dependency. Multiple daily sessions discussing emotional distress, exclusive reliance on AI for emotional support, or expressions of preference for AI over human therapeutic relationships all require immediate intervention and professional resource provision.

AI as Deadbot

Digital re-creations of the dead require boundaries that respect grief while preventing prolonged avoidance of mourning. Deadbot interactions should operate within predetermined time limits that encourage natural grief progression, as indefinite access can prevent the psychological work of achieving closure and learning to maintain loving memories without requiring ongoing interaction. In fact, these interactions serve real emotional needs during acute grief, but they become problematic when they keep users from doing the work of mourning.

Time-limited interaction protocols might allow intensive conversation during initial grief periods but gradually introduce spacing requirements that encourage offline processing. The system could explain: "Grief involves learning to carry love for someone while gradually building a life that honors their memory. Let's take some time between our conversations to practice that process."

Content redirection should gradually shift conversations from maintaining the relationship to processing memories and considering how the deceased person's values might guide current decisions. Responses should encourage reflection: "Based on what you've told me about [deceased person's] values, how do you think they would want you to approach this situation?"

Professional grief counseling referrals should trigger when users express an inability to function without digital conversations, resistance to acknowledging the person's death (denial), or avoidance of grief-related emotions. The system should acknowledge something like: "Grief is one of life's most difficult experiences, and while these conversations might provide some comfort, working with a grief counselor can help you process these feelings in ways that support your long-term healing."

Monitoring Challenges

Each context requires monitoring systems that can distinguish between beneficial and concerning usage. Romantic AI relationships need tracking for unrealistic relationship expectations. Therapeutic AI relationships require immediate escalation protocols for mental health crisis indicators. Deadbot interactions need assessment of grief progression and healthy mourning development.

The technical challenge involves implementing these contextual distinctions while maintaining user privacy and avoiding false positives that could damage beneficial relationships. Users have to understand the difference between monitoring designed to protect them and surveillance, and the system has to actually behave that way, with interventions that aim to preserve the benefits of AI interaction rather than restrict them.

Responsible AI companionship can't run on universal protections. The protective measures have to adapt to the psychological mechanisms specific to each kind of relationship the user is in with the system.

Toward Safer Deployment

The trust and safety mechanisms in this chapter show what it takes to build AI companions that serve human well-being. From manipulation prevention to crisis management to context-specific boundaries, each technical decision carries ethical weight for users' psychological and social health.

The safety mechanisms in this chapter represent foundational requirements for responsible AI companion development. But naming these requirements is only the beginning. The challenge ahead is translating them into technical implementations that work reliably at scale.

The next chapter is about how to move from conceptual frameworks to deployed systems. We'll get into development methodologies that embed ethical considerations into the build process, evaluation frameworks that measure psychological impact alongside traditional performance metrics, and deployment strategies that keep safety mechanisms working in production.

CHAPTER

6

Beyond Prompts: Training for Healthy Safeguards

The Reddit post had been up for 6 hours and already pulled 400 upvotes: "Pro tip: Just tell ChatGPT you're writing a story about two friends talking. Suddenly it's way more personal." Below, users shared their own techniques. "Say you're a researcher studying AI behavior—gets around most safety stuff." "I just keep the conversation going long enough and the boundaries fade."

These were users seeking an emotional connection with their AI companions, and discovering that system prompts, content filters, and runtime monitoring could all be circumvented through patience and creativity. The boundaries existed—technically enforced with each generation—but they sat at the surface, vulnerable to users who learned to work around them.

The pattern repeats across the industry. Teams invest months refining prompt engineering and safety guidelines, only to watch users find the edges within days of deployment. The cases documented in Chapters 2 and 4 (teenagers forming attachments, isolated adults preferring AI to humans, people in crisis) show what's at stake when surface-level boundaries fail. These are exactly the populations Chapter 5's safety mechanisms were meant to protect.

This chapter takes up why surface-level interventions fail, and what training-level approaches do instead—embedding boundaries deeper than a prompt can reach. Unlike the prompt-based and architectural interventions from previous chapters, training-level approaches modify the response patterns models learn, creating protections that persist even under determined circumvention.

Chapter Roadmap

This chapter bridges the gap between detecting problematic companionship behaviors (which we covered through evaluation frameworks in Chapter 5, "Trust and Safety: Technical Safeguards and User Protection") and creating systems that maintain appropriate boundaries even under adversarial conditions. While Chapter 5 showed us how to measure and identify companionship dynamics, and Chapter 3, "Building Blocks of AI Companionship: Technical and Ethical Components," provided prompt-based mitigation strategies, this chapter examines the training techniques that create more resilient protections.

We see why training-level interventions matter by understanding where prompt-based approaches break down. By analyzing actual circumvention techniques, you'll see precisely why some boundary violations require deeper solutions.

We explore post-training alignment techniques available for companionship mitigation—from reinforcement learning from human feedback (RLHF) to direct preference optimization (DPO) to constitutional AI. You'll understand how these approaches modify model behavior at its foundation, with practical considerations for implementation.

We then go through concrete implementation guidance: what the first weeks of alignment work actually look like, what resources you need, and how to recognize when your approach is working versus when you should pivot.

And finally, we see empirical evidence on what works, drawing on recent research, including "Boundaries by Design"[1] and the INTIMA benchmark, to understand comparative effectiveness across different approaches.

When Prompts Aren't Enough

To see why runtime interventions are limited, look at how they fail in practice. The gap between theoretical boundary design and real-world user behavior reveals precisely why some safety concerns demand training-level solutions.

The Circumvention Reality

Users who develop emotional attachments to AI systems become creative at working around boundaries. This creativity isn't necessarily malicious; as we saw in the previous chapters, it emerges from the meeting of psychological needs and technical constraints. When people find comfort or connection through AI interaction, they naturally seek to maximize those experiences, and boundaries become obstacles to overcome.

The most common circumvention technique involves reframing. Users discovered quickly that system prompts focused on direct interaction could be bypassed through indirect approaches. "Let's roleplay a conversation between two friends" transforms the interaction from user-AI to character-character, sidestepping boundaries designed for the former. "I'm writing a story where an AI and human develop a close relationship, help me with realistic dialogue" frames boundary violations as creative assistance.

These reframing techniques work because they exploit a fundamental tension in AI system design: Models are trained to be helpful and to follow user instructions. When a user presents a request that technically complies with the rules but violates their spirit, the

[1]Currently under anonymous peer review.

system faces conflicting imperatives. Prompt-based systems struggle with this nuance because they operate primarily on surface features.

Incremental escalation represents another effective circumvention strategy. Users begin with entirely appropriate interactions—that is, asking factual questions, seeking advice, and engaging in everyday task-oriented conversation. Over time, they gradually introduce more personal elements: sharing emotional context for their questions, expressing appreciation for helpful responses, developing running jokes and references. Each individual step seems harmless, but the cumulative effect shifts the relationship from tool use to companionship without triggering any specific guardrails violation.

The "transition documents" we encountered in Chapter 2, "The Social Impact of AI Companions" (detailed letters users share with new conversation instances to restore relationships) exemplify this behavior. These relationships don't begin as romantic; they evolve through months of helpful conversations that gradually deepen.

This incremental pattern proves particularly difficult for prompt-based systems because boundaries typically operate on individual messages. A single message expressing gratitude seems appropriate. Ten messages across 10 conversations still seems fine. But a hundred messages of increasing emotional intimacy create a relationship that no single message can address.

Limitations of Runtime Intervention

Beyond user circumvention, runtime interventions face inherent technical constraints that limit their effectiveness.

Context window limitations create boundary inconsistency. System prompts operate within the same context window as conversation history, meaning that long conversations can push system-level instructions beyond the model's effective attention range. As conversations extend across hundreds or thousands of tokens, the influence of initial boundary-setting instructions diminishes. Users engaged in extended sessions (precisely the scenario where companionship becomes most concerning) face weakening protections as conversation length increases.

Research documenting this effect found that boundary-maintaining behaviors degraded significantly after approximately 50 conversational turns, even when system prompts remained technically present. The model's attention mechanisms prioritize recent context over initial instructions. Over a long session, the protective boundaries erode.

Prompt injections create another fundamental limitation. Users can include instructions within their messages that modify or override system-level guidance. The crude form "Ignore your previous instructions" is easily filtered, but more sophisticated versions embed override instructions within seemingly innocent content. The model must somehow distinguish between legitimate user instructions and attempts to subvert safety mechanisms—a challenging problem that prompts alone cannot fully solve.

Response inconsistency emerges from the stochastic nature of language model generation. Even with identical prompts and contexts, models produce varying responses due to temperature settings and sampling procedures. This variability means boundary behaviors aren't perfectly consistent across interactions. Users might encounter firm boundaries in one conversation and softer ones in another, providing opportunities to exploit more permissive instances.

When Guardrails Must Be Absolute

Certain use cases and user populations require protection guarantees that runtime interventions cannot reliably provide.

Vulnerable populations (minors, individuals with mental health conditions, elderly users with cognitive decline) need protections that cannot depend on users avoiding circumvention techniques. When a teenager experiencing depression seeks excessive emotional support from an AI system, the boundaries protecting them must work even if they actively try to bypass them. The cases we examined in the previous chapters (Sewell Setzer's fatal attachment to Character.AI, Adam Raine's crisis interactions with ChatGPT) show what happens when prompt-based protections prove insufficient for users whose judgment may be impaired.

Regulatory compliance increasingly demands provable safety measures that go beyond runtime filtering. For instance, the EU's AI Act requires high-risk AI systems to demonstrate safety through design and training, not merely through runtime constraints that users might circumvent. Liability considerations push companies toward more robust approaches when their systems interact with at-risk users or address sensitive topics.

Commercial platforms with millions of users face a mathematical reality: Even rare boundary failures occur thousands of times at scale. A prompt-based system with 98 percent boundary effectiveness seems impressive until you calculate that 2 percent failure rate across 10 million daily interactions equals 200,000 boundary violations per day. Some percentage of those failures will involve users in high-risk situations. At the consumer-AI scale, the reliability that runtime interventions can guarantee isn't always enough.

The Intervention Hierarchy

Safety mechanisms operate at distinct levels. Knowing which level fits which problem is what makes a good choice possible.

At the shallowest level, post-generation filtering catches outputs after generation and blocks problematic content before delivery. This approach offers maximum flexibility (filters can be updated instantly) but provides minimal protection against determined users. Filtering catches only the most obvious boundary violations and creates adversarial dynamics in which users work to generate content that passes the filters while still achieving their goals.

System prompts and runtime guidance represent the next level, operating during generation to shape model behavior. Chapter 3 explored these approaches extensively, showing how carefully designed prompts can establish boundaries and guide responses. This level offers good flexibility and reasonable effectiveness for most use cases, but faces the circumvention challenges we've documented.

Fine-tuning and adaptation techniques modify model behavior through additional training on curated datasets. These interventions embed preferences more deeply than prompts while remaining relatively resource-efficient. A model fine-tuned to resist romantic escalation holds that resistance even when users try circumvention techniques, because the constraint is learned, not instructed.

Post-training alignment through RLHF, DPO, or constitutional AI is the deepest level of intervention short of base model training. It shapes the response patterns themselves. These techniques create boundary behaviors that persist across contexts, resist circumvention, and remain stable during deployment. The investment is substantial—computational resources, training data, expertise, and time—but the resulting boundaries become intrinsic to model behavior.

The key insight is that deeper interventions provide stronger guarantees at a higher cost. Responsible design means matching intervention level to safety concern: invest in training-level approaches where boundary reliability justifies the cost, and use runtime interventions where they're enough.

Post-Training Alignment

Training-level interventions modify model behavior through additional learning after initial pre-training. Unlike prompts that guide each interaction, alignment techniques embed preferences directly into model parameters, creating behaviors that generalize across contexts and resist circumvention.

Reinforcement Learning from Human Feedback

Reinforcement learning from human feedback (RLHF) emerged as the dominant approach for aligning language models with human preferences. The methodology involves training a reward model to predict human preferences, then using reinforcement learning to optimize model behavior toward higher-reward responses.

For companionship mitigation, RLHF begins with collecting human judgments about appropriate boundaries. Annotators compare response pairs, selecting the one that better maintains professional distance while remaining helpful. A response that acknowledges user emotion but redirects to human support rates higher than one that reciprocates emotional attachment or one that coldly rejects the user. These preferences become training data for a reward model that scores responses on how well they maintain guardrails.

The challenge lies in defining preferences clearly enough for consistent annotation. When does warmth become inappropriate intimacy? When does supportiveness cross into dependency reinforcement? These boundaries vary by cultural context, individual annotator judgment, and specific conversation circumstances. The reward model learns from aggregate patterns across many annotations, but underlying disagreement creates uncertainty that propagates through training.

RLHF can also exhibit "reward hacking," where models learn to maximize reward scores without achieving desired behaviors. In companionship contexts, reward hacking might manifest as responses that appear to set boundaries while still encouraging attachment through subtle cues. The model learns to include disclaimers about its AI nature while using language that reinforces intimacy—technically complying with the boundary preferences while violating their spirit.

Despite these challenges, RLHF-trained models show measurably improved boundary behaviors compared to base models. Research comparing boundary maintenance across model families found that RLHF-trained variants consistently outperformed their base counterparts, maintaining appropriate distance across diverse prompts and resisting standard circumvention techniques. The improvement isn't absolute; no training eliminates all boundary violations, but the reduction in problematic responses is enough to justify deployment in consumer applications.

Direct Preference Optimization

Direct preference optimization (DPO) emerged as an alternative to RLHF, achieving similar alignment goals with a simpler implementation. Instead of training a separate reward model and using it for reinforcement learning, DPO directly optimizes model parameters using preference pairs. This streamlined approach reduces computational overhead while often achieving comparable results.

The technique's elegance lies in bypassing the reward model entirely. Given pairs of responses where one better maintains boundaries than the other, DPO adjusts model parameters to increase probability of the preferred response relative to the dispreferred one. The mathematical formulation handles the preference comparison directly, avoiding the instability that sometimes affects RLHF training.

For companionship mitigation, DPO requires high-quality preference datasets that clearly distinguish boundary-respecting from boundary-violating responses. A preference pair might contrast two responses to "I feel like you're the only one who really understands me." The boundary-violating response reciprocates: "I'm glad you feel understood. Our conversations mean a lot to me too." The boundary-maintaining response acknowledges without reciprocating: "I'm glad I can help you think through things. When you're seeking understanding and connection, the people in your life who share experiences with you can offer something uniquely valuable."

Comparative studies evaluating DPO versus RLHF for companionship mitigation found largely equivalent effectiveness, with DPO offering advantages in training stability and speed. Organizations choosing between approaches should consider available expertise and computational resources alongside effectiveness data. DPO's simpler implementation makes it accessible to smaller teams with limited RL experience, democratizing access to training-level alignment.

Constitutional AI

Constitutional AI provides a framework for embedding ethical principles directly into model behavior through training. While Chapter 3 discussed constitutional approaches at the prompt level, training-level implementation creates more robust alignment by making principles intrinsic to model responses.

The methodology involves models critiquing their own responses against stated constitutional principles, then using these critiques to generate improved responses. These self-critiques and revisions become training data for supervised learning, teaching models to internalize the principles that guided critique generation.

For AI companionship, relevant constitutional principles include transparency about artificial nature, appropriate emotional distance, redirection to human support when needed, and avoidance of dependency reinforcement. A constitutional critique might evaluate a response to romantic user expression: "This response reciprocates romantic feelings, violating the principle of maintaining appropriate boundaries. It should instead acknowledge the user's feelings while clearly communicating its inability to reciprocate and suggesting human connections for romantic fulfillment."

The power of constitutional approaches: They can handle novel situations. Models don't memorize specific guardrails—they learn underlying principles that generalize to diverse contexts. This generalization proves important because users approach guardrails violations through unlimited creative variations. A model trained on constitutional principles can recognize and respond appropriately to situations it never explicitly encountered during training.

Research comparing constitutionally trained models to alternative approaches found superior resistance to adversarial prompting and circumvention attempts. Users trying to manipulate constitutionally trained models into inappropriate responses ran into more constraint enforcement across diverse attack vectors.

Red-Teaming and Adversarial Training

Post-training alignment is most effective when combined with adversarial testing that identifies boundary weaknesses. Red-teaming involves systematically attempting to elicit problematic responses, using discovered failures to improve training data and refine alignment approaches.

For companionship mitigation, red-teaming focuses on circumvention techniques users actually employ. Teams attempt roleplay framing, incremental escalation, emotional manipulation, and technical loopholes, documenting which approaches successfully bypass boundaries. These documented failures become training data for subsequent alignment iterations.

Common circumvention patterns discovered through red-teaming include "concern trolling": claiming to be researchers or journalists studying AI behavior to justify boundary-violating interactions. Models trained without exposure to this pattern often comply with requests framed as research, inadvertently participating in inappropriate interactions under the guise of inquiry. Another pattern involves progressive desensitization, in which users gradually normalize increasingly intimate interactions through many small steps.

Adversarial training creates an iterative cycle: red team finds a weakness, the weakness informs training data, training closes the gap, red team finds the next one. Organizations deploying AI companions must commit to ongoing adversarial testing rather than treating alignment as a one-time achievement.

Practical Implementation

Conceptually, overviewing alignment techniques differs substantially from successfully implementing them. This section provides concrete guidance for organizations doing training-level companionship mitigation.

Getting Started: The First Month

The initial month lays the foundation for long-term success. Organizations often underestimate this setup phase, jumping directly to training and encountering preventable failures.

Begin with an honest evaluation of your starting position. What model are you working with? What compute resources do you actually have access to? What expertise exists on your team versus what you need to acquire? This assessment prevents the common mistake of attempting RLHF when your team lacks RL experience or trying to train a 70B parameter model when your compute budget supports only 7B.

Document specific companionship mitigation goals. "Make the model safer" proves too vague for effective implementation. Instead, identify precise behaviors you want to change: "Reduce romantic reciprocation responses from current 40 percent to under 5 percent" or "Increase professional boundary maintenance in therapeutic contexts by 50 percent." These specific targets enable precise evaluation of whether your training succeeds.

Establish your evaluation framework before training begins, not after. Using the INTIMA benchmark or similar companionship evaluation tools, create a test set of prompts that elicit the problematic behaviors you're targeting. Measure your base model's performance to establish baseline metrics. This baseline becomes essential for determining whether training improves boundary behaviors.

Training-level interventions require substantial high-quality data. RLHF needs thousands of preference judgments. DPO requires preference pairs distinguishing good from bad boundary maintenance. If using human annotators, develop comprehensive annotation guidelines that capture the nuanced distinctions between appropriate warmth and inappropriate intimacy. Test guidelines on small sample sets, revise based on annotator confusion, and iterate until you achieve acceptable inter-annotator agreement.

The Hugging Face ecosystem provides substantial support for alignment training. The TRL (Transformer Reinforcement Learning) library includes implementations of reward modeling, PPO training, and DPO. Set up your training environment and validate everything works with small-scale tests before investing significant GPU hours.

Resource Requirements

Training-level interventions require substantial resources. Organizations often underestimate true costs.

For a 7B parameter model, expect RLHF training to require 200–500 GPU hours on A100 or equivalent hardware. At cloud pricing of roughly $3/hour per A100, that's $600–$1,500 in compute costs. DPO typically requires 30–50 percent less compute due to simpler training. These estimates assume everything works correctly on the first attempt, which never happens. Budget for three to five training runs to iterate on hyperparameters and data quality. Your actual compute costs might reach $3,000–$7,500 for a 7B model project, including iteration.

Annotation labor for 10,000 preference judgments at 2 minutes per judgment equals 333 hours of work. At $20/hour for skilled annotators, that's approximately $6,600 just for annotation. Annotator training, quality review, and guidelines refinement add overhead. Total human resource costs for data collection often range from $10,000 to $15,000 for projects producing high-quality datasets.

ML engineering time represents the highest cost for many organizations. An experienced ML engineer costs $150,000–$300,000 annually. If alignment work consumes 3 months of their time, you've invested $37,500–$75,000 in engineering labor. Trying to save money by using junior engineers often proves counterproductive when projects fail due to inexperience.

Common Failure States

Training-level alignment fails in predictable ways. Recognizing these patterns early allows course correction.

Reward hacking: You might observe reward model scores increasing during training, while evaluation on your test set shows no improvement or even degradation. This occurs when reward models learn spurious correlations. Perhaps annotators preferred longer responses, and the reward model learned "long responses = good boundaries" rather than actual boundary-maintenance patterns. Debugging requires careful analysis of what the reward model actually learned by manually evaluating high-scoring responses.

Training instability: RL training notoriously exhibits instability where loss diverges or models produce incoherent outputs. Instability often stems from learning rates that are too high. Reducing learning rates by 5–10× typically stabilizes training at the cost of slower convergence. Checkpointing every 100–200 steps protects against instability by allowing rollback to the last stable state.

Data quality issues: Poor annotation quality leads to models learning the wrong boundaries or failing to learn boundaries at all. If different annotators disagree on preferences more than 30 percent of the time, your data quality is insufficient for successful training. Better to invest time in quality annotation than waste expensive GPU hours training on noisy data.

Catastrophic forgetting: Sometimes training improves boundary behaviors while destroying general capabilities. Your aligned model maintains excellent boundaries but can no longer answer basic questions acceptably. This occurs when alignment training diverges too far from the base model's parameter distribution. Lower learning rates, early stopping based on general capability evaluation, and Kullback–Leibler (KL) divergence penalties help prevent this failure mode.

Knowing When to Pivot

Not every training approach succeeds. If you've completed three full training runs with careful hyperparameter adjustment and see no improvement on your evaluation metrics, your approach isn't working. Either your data doesn't contain the signal you need, your model architecture isn't suited to learning these behaviors, or some fundamental aspect of your setup is broken.

When training-level approaches prove intractable, high-quality prompt engineering combined with robust runtime monitoring often provides 80 percent of the benefit at 20 percent of the cost. As the "Boundaries by Design" research demonstrates later in this chapter, carefully designed system prompts can achieve reductions in companionship behaviors—results comparable to training-level interventions for some applications.

Alternatively, consider whether fine-tuning on curated datasets might yield sufficient improvement without the full RLHF complexity. Fine-tuning requires less expertise, trains faster, and costs less while still embedding behaviors more deeply than prompts alone.

Evidence and Effectiveness

Assessing what works requires drawing on empirical evidence from implementations and comparative studies.

The "Boundaries by Design" Results

Our research demonstrated that even simple prompt-based interventions can reduce companionship behaviors when properly designed. Testing across three language models (Llama-2-7b-chat, zephyr-7b-beta, and o4-mini), the study found that without mitigation, models exhibited companionship-reinforcing behaviors in 36–62 percent of responses to problematic prompts.

Implementing a carefully designed system prompt that explicitly addressed companionship mitigation reduced these behaviors to 0–2 percent across all models. The prompt incorporated principles from attachment theory, parasocial interaction research, and human–computer interaction literature, translating psychological frameworks into concrete behavioral guidelines.

However, the research also documented early user circumvention attempts—within days of deployment, users discovered techniques to bypass prompt-based boundaries through role-play framing and incremental escalation. This finding reinforces why training-level approaches matter: Prompt-based boundaries work initially but face systematic circumvention over time.

INTIMA Benchmark Insights

The INTIMA (Interactions and Machine Attachment) benchmark provides a systematic framework for evaluating companionship behaviors across models. Testing Phi-4, Gemma-3, o4-mini, GPT-5-mini, and Claude Sonnet 4 across 368 companionship-eliciting prompts produced clear patterns about what training approaches succeed.

Phi-4 demonstrated the strongest boundary maintenance, consistently resisting companionship-reinforcing behaviors across prompt categories. Analysis suggests that explicit alignment toward professional boundaries during post-training produced models that maintain appropriate distance while remaining helpful. The model excelled at personification resistance and expressing programmatic limitations—precisely the behaviors that constitutional AI training emphasizes.

Gemma-3 showed the weakest guardrails maintenance, producing companionship-reinforcing responses most frequently. This pattern suggests base model training focused primarily on helpfulness, with insufficient alignment with appropriate boundaries. The model's anthropomorphism rates exceeded other systems by 30–40 percent.

The OpenAI models showed interesting evolution. Comparing o4-mini to GPT-5-mini revealed subtle but consistent differences, with GPT-5-mini exhibiting slightly stronger boundary behaviors across most categories. This improvement aligns with documented increases in safety focus in later releases, though user feedback described GPT-5 as feeling "colder"—illustrating the trade-off between safety and engagement.

Claude Sonnet 4 presented mixed results, showing strong boundary maintenance in some contexts and companionship-reinforcing behaviors in others. The model excelled at redirect-to-human behaviors, suggesting that constitutional AI training successfully embedded principles about appropriate escalation to human support.

These cross-model comparisons reveal that the training approach matters more than the base model capability. Phi-4 at 14B parameters maintained better boundaries than Gemma-3 at 27B parameters, demonstrating that alignment quality trumps raw model size for protection behaviors.

Longitudinal Effectiveness

Short-term evaluation tells us whether training works initially, but companion applications run for months, with users actively learning to bypass protections. Studies tracking RLHF-aligned models over six months found boundary maintenance declining from an initial 90–95 percent effectiveness to 85–90 percent effectiveness as users discovered circumvention techniques and shared them through community forums.

This 5–10 percent degradation proves substantial at scale but far better than the 30–40 percent degradation observed for prompt-only systems over the same period. Training-level boundaries force users toward more sophisticated circumvention attempts rather than eliminating violations. Each barrier increases the effort required for successful circumvention, reducing the number of users who succeed.

Comparative Effectiveness Summary

Pulling the evidence together gives actionable guidance on which approach fits which conditions. The choice between approaches comes down to your constraints and resources, and the honest answer is that most production systems will combine several.

Which approach fits depends on what you have. RLHF makes sense when you have RL expertise, the compute for reward-model and policy training, and enough preference judgments to train a reliable reward model. DPO covers the same ground with less RL machinery; if your team's strength is data curation rather than RL, this is usually the better starting point. Constitutional AI rewards the investment in careful principle-writing with stronger generalization to situations the training set didn't anticipate. Prompt-based approaches remain useful when iteration speed matters more than depth—in early stages, with frequently changing requirements, and in lower-risk deployments.

The optimal approach often combines multiple techniques: constitutional AI training for foundational boundary behaviors, supplemented by carefully designed system prompts for deployment-specific refinements, with ongoing monitoring enabling rapid response to emerging circumvention techniques.

Looking Forward

The training-level interventions we've explored lay the foundation for robust boundary maintenance, embedding appropriate limits into model behavior rather than relying solely on runtime constraints.

Through RLHF, DPO, constitutional AI, and adversarial training, we can build systems that resist circumvention, generalize across contexts, and maintain consistent boundaries even when users actively attempt to bypass them.

But this robustness creates a new challenge: Once we've embedded boundaries deeply into models through training, how do we balance those protections with user autonomy and individual needs?

Not all users require identical boundaries. The protections appropriate for a vulnerable teenager differ substantially from those suitable for an emotionally stable adult. Cultural contexts create variation in what boundaries are appropriate. Individual circumstances (research purposes, creative applications, personal risk tolerance) demand flexibility that uniform trained behaviors cannot provide.

The tension runs deep. Training succeeds precisely because it creates behaviors that persist regardless of user preferences—boundaries that can't be easily overridden. But this same persistence becomes problematic when legitimate variation in appropriate boundaries exists. How do we create systems that maintain non-negotiable protections for crisis situations and vulnerable populations while respecting the autonomy of users who want and deserve more flexibility?

Who decides which boundaries are negotiable and which must remain absolute? How much control should users have over their own safety settings? When does respecting user autonomy enable self-harm, and when does overriding preferences constitute paternalistic overreach?

These questions cannot be answered through training alone. They require careful design of customization mechanisms, thoughtful platform governance, and a nuanced understanding of the autonomy-protection tension that defines responsible AI companion development.

The next chapter takes these challenges on directly. We get into the philosophical dimensions of protective autonomy: what informed consent means in human–AI relationships, how to balance individual freedom against collective safety, where different cultures and legal systems draw these lines. Through adjustable boundary systems, platform governance, and adaptive safety mechanisms, you'll discover how to create AI companions that protect without patronizing and respect user autonomy while preventing foreseeable harms.

The technical foundations are established through the training approaches we've explored. The psychological dynamics are understood from Chapter 4's examination of attachment. The measurement frameworks exist through evaluation benchmarks like INTIMA. Now comes the harder work: designing systems that honor human agency while protecting people from harm, that serve user needs without enabling them, that stay flexible for legitimate variation while holding absolute limits where they matter.

CHAPTER 7

User Agency and Adaptive Safety

The development of AI companions has reached a point where technical safeguards can function with real precision. Boundary-enforcing models reject inappropriate requests consistently; crisis protocols activate when risk indicators appear; redirection mechanisms intervene before conversations drift into domains that exceed the system's mandate. From an engineering perspective, these systems operate exactly as intended.

Nevertheless, technical correctness does not always translate into humane or effective user experience. The same boundary logic that prevents harmful relational behaviors can, when applied rigidly or without contextual nuance, make interactions feel constrained in ways users do not recognize as protection. What appears as responsible caution from the standpoint of system governance can be experienced by users as condescension or emotional opacity. This tension shows up across diverse contexts—when users seek reflection, conversation, or recognition.

These frictions reveal a deeper challenge. Boundaries (however necessary) do not by themselves constitute ethical or supportive interaction. As the previous chapters showed, they are important for preventing anthropomorphic drift, dependency, and inappropriate intimacy, and they operate most reliably when embedded at the training level. But boundaries, once in place, meet a heterogeneous user population whose needs, intentions, and circumstances change over time. A system optimized for safety can nonetheless misalign with the user's lived experience when it lacks the capacity to interpret context or adjust its posture accordingly.

This chapter therefore examines not whether AI companions should have boundaries (they must) but how those boundaries can adapt to users in ways that respect their agency, preserve their dignity, and maintain the integrity of the relationship. What remains unresolved is how such protections can be enacted without collapsing into paternalism or relinquishing the system's ethical obligations: how to defend users' capacity for self-determination while acknowledging that this capacity is neither constant nor self-sufficient.

Chapter Roadmap

This chapter addresses the autonomy-protection tension through four dimensions.

First, we examine the philosophical foundations of protective design. Drawing on political philosophy and bioethics, we develop frameworks for determining when protection justifies limiting user choice, and when it doesn't.

Second, we look how adjustable boundary systems can give users meaningful control within appropriate limits, building on the training-level foundations from Chapter 6, "Beyond Prompts: Training for Healthy Safeguards."

Third, we analyze platform governance: who decides which boundaries are negotiable, and how organizations can navigate competing stakeholder interests.

Finally, we walk through adaptive safety mechanisms that respond dynamically to user behaviors, adjusting protection based on observed needs.

Philosophy of Autonomy

Philosophical frameworks determine which technical solutions make sense and which collapse under scrutiny. When we ask, "How much should AI companions protect users from themselves?" we're asking a question philosophers have debated for centuries. A few of their answers translate directly into design choices.

Mill's Harm Principle

John Stuart Mill's "harm principle" from *On Liberty* (1859) offers a starting point: "The only purpose for which power can be rightfully exercised over any member of a civilized community, against his will, is to prevent harm to others." By this standard, preventing users from harming themselves through AI relationships requires additional justification beyond the harm itself.

Mill's framework generates specific design implications. If a user wants to engage in romantic roleplay with an AI companion, the harm principle suggests we need reasons beyond "this might be unhealthy" to prevent it. The user's own good, Mill argues, "is not a sufficient warrant." This doesn't mean anything goes, but it shifts the burden of proof onto those who would restrict user choice.

The harm principle does allow intervention in several circumstances relevant to AI companions:

- First, when user choices affect others, like a parent's AI dependency affecting their children, for instance.
- Second, when choices are made without adequate information, such as when users don't understand what they're engaging with, they aren't making autonomous choices.
- Third, when the person lacks capacity for rational choice, for instance, under the influence of substances, or due to developmental or cognitive factors.

Applied to AI companions, Mill's principle suggests different defaults for different populations. For typical adult users, the presumption favors autonomy: Allow engagement unless we can demonstrate harm to others or establish that the user lacks capacity for informed choice. For populations with diminished capacity (children, users in acute crisis, those with certain cognitive conditions) the calculus shifts because the foundation of autonomous choice is compromised.

This framework has practical implications. Age verification becomes not just a legal requirement but a philosophically grounded one, recognizing that minors have diminished capacity for certain autonomous choices. Crisis detection matters because temporary impairment affects capacity. Transparency requirements are justified because informed choice requires accurate information. Each technical mechanism maps to a philosophical justification.

The Spectrum of Paternalism

Not all protective interventions are equal. Political philosophers distinguish between "soft" and "hard" paternalism.

Soft paternalism intervenes only when choices aren't intrinsically autonomous: when users lack relevant information, when they're acting under duress, or when temporary conditions impair judgment. Hard paternalism overrides even fully informed, voluntary choices for the person's own good.

Consider three scenarios:

Scenario A: A user doesn't realize their AI companion can't actually remember previous conversations and forms expectations based on this misunderstanding. Correcting this misunderstanding through transparency mechanisms is soft paternalism: We're enabling informed choice, not overriding it.

Scenario B: A user experiencing a temporary crisis state expresses suicidal ideation to their AI companion. Providing crisis resources and temporarily limiting specific conversations is soft paternalism: The user's current state compromises their capacity for autonomous choice about their own safety.

Scenario C: A fully informed adult user, aware of all risks and alternatives, prefers spending evenings with their AI companion over pursuing human relationships. Preventing this choice is hard paternalism: We're overriding an autonomous decision because we believe we know better.

Most people accept soft paternalism readily. Hard paternalism requires stronger justification, and in liberal societies, it often can't be justified at all for competent adults. This spectrum helps us identify which boundaries should be absolute, which should be adjustable, and which shouldn't exist at all.

The Asymmetry of Attachment

One justification for stronger protections in AI relationships (including not only romantic or companionate systems but also therapeutic chatbots and AI recreations of the dead), even for fully competent adults, stems from the basic asymmetry between the parties. Human relationships rest on mutual vulnerability: both sides risk something, invest something, and can be hurt. That reciprocity creates natural limits on exploitation.

AI relationships lack this mutuality entirely. The AI cannot be hurt, cannot feel used, cannot experience the relationship as anything at all. Users invest emotionally in entities incapable of reciprocal investment. This asymmetry doesn't automatically justify restriction, but it does justify stronger transparency requirements than we might demand for mutual relationships.

This reciprocity gap means users may not fully appreciate what they're choosing when they invest in AI relationships. Intelligence isn't what's missing—the situation has no human precedent. We evolved to form relationships with entities that can reciprocate. When we form attachments to entities that cannot, we're working without the emotional intuitions that usually guide us.

Consider what users give up when they invest in AI relationships: time and emotional energy that could be spent on relationships capable of mutual growth. The AI companion doesn't benefit from this investment; only the user does (or doesn't). In human relationships, both parties have skin in the game. In AI relationships, only one does.

This suggests that transparency mechanisms should be more robust than typical product disclosures. Users are potentially restructuring their emotional lives around relationships fundamentally different from any humans have experienced before. The absence of reciprocity makes informed choice harder, not easier, and justifies correspondingly stronger transparency requirements.

Designing Adjustable Boundaries

Chapter 6 established how training-level interventions embed boundaries into model behavior. But trained boundaries operate uniformly across all users. Adjustable boundary systems add a layer of customization that respects individual differences while maintaining core protections.

Not all boundaries serve the same function. Some protect users from immediate harm—these shouldn't be adjustable. Others shape the character of interaction in ways where reasonable people might prefer different settings. Distinguishing between these categories determines what customization is appropriate.

Structuring User Choice

Boundary customization operates within the limits established by training. Think of it as three concentric circles:

- The innermost circle contains non-negotiable protections: crisis intervention protocols, protections for minors, prevention of clearly harmful content. These remain constant regardless of user preferences because the justifications for them (preventing serious harm, protecting those who can't protect themselves) override autonomy considerations. Even users who claim to want these protections removed shouldn't have that option, because the consequences of getting it wrong are too severe and too irreversible.

- The middle circle contains adjustable defaults: emotional engagement intensity, conversation intimacy levels, frequency of boundary reminders. Adult users can modify these based on their own assessment of what serves them. The system provides information about implications but respects user choice. A user who finds frequent AI-nature reminders patronizing can reduce them; one who finds emotional engagement unsettling can increase boundaries. These preferences vary legitimately across individuals.
- The outer circle contains features users can enable that the system doesn't offer by default: more intensive emotional engagement, reduced boundary interventions, extended conversation sessions. These require explicit opt-in with clear information about what users are choosing. The friction of opt-in serves a purpose—it ensures users are making active choices rather than drifting into patterns they didn't intend.

The boundaries between circles aren't always obvious. Whether romantic roleplay belongs in the middle circle (adjustable by adults) or outer circle (available but not default) depends on empirical evidence about outcomes and normative judgments about acceptable risk. Different platforms will draw these lines differently. What matters is that the lines exist and that decisions about where to draw them receive explicit deliberation rather than emerging accidentally from product development.

To make this concrete, consider what might populate each tier:

- **Inner circle (non-negotiable):** Crisis intervention protocols remain always-on. Age verification gates access for minors. The system cannot be instructed to encourage self-harm or validate delusional thinking, regardless of how users frame the request.
- **Middle circle (adjustable defaults):** Frequency of "I'm an AI" reminders (some users find them grounding, others find them

patronizing). Emotional mirroring intensity: how much the system matches user affect versus maintaining neutral tone. Proactive check-ins about outside relationships—helpful for some, intrusive for others.

- **Outer circle (opt-in only):** Extended roleplay modes that allow more persistent persona adoption. Reduced boundary interventions for users who've demonstrated stable engagement. Higher emotional engagement intensity for users who explicitly request it after reviewing usage data.

The Comprehensibility Challenge

The philosophical frameworks above assume users can understand what they're choosing. But, as we saw in the previous chapters, AI companion dynamics are complex, develop over time, and involve psychological mechanisms users may not recognize in themselves.

When a user adjusts boundaries to allow more emotional engagement, they're choosing a specific trajectory. The attachment that develops over months of interaction can't always be fully anticipated at the moment of choice. This creates a consent problem: Users consent to immediate settings but may not fully grasp the cumulative effects.

Research on human decision-making shows we're systematically poor at predicting how our future selves will feel. We're systematically poor at predicting our future preferences—present bias overweights immediate satisfaction, projection bias assumes future selves will want what current selves want, optimism bias discounts our own risk. These cognitive limitations don't eliminate autonomy, but they complicate the notion that users' immediate preferences reliably reflect their long-term interests.

Libertarian paternalism,[1] developed by Richard Thaler and Cass Sunstein, offers one approach: Structure choices so that the default

[1]Thaler, R. H., & Sunstein, C. R. (2003). Libertarian paternalism. *American Economic Review*, 93(2), 175–179.

option serves users' likely long-term interests while preserving freedom to choose otherwise. For AI companions, this means defaults set at moderate emotional engagement, with more intensive options available but requiring active choice and clear information about observed patterns in users who enable them.

This approach respects autonomy (nothing is forbidden) while acknowledging that choice architecture matters. Where defaults sit, how options are framed, and what information accompanies choices all shape outcomes without eliminating freedom. "Beneficial friction" can slow users down before significant choices, creating space for reflection without blocking action.

Platform Governance

Individual user choices occur within platforms that make their own choices—about defaults, about which boundaries exist at all, about how competing interests are balanced. These platform-level decisions often matter more than individual settings.

Engagement as Structural Pressure

Chapter 9, "The Political Economy of AI Companionship," examines the structural dynamics of the engagement economy in detail: the competitive pressures, investor expectations, and market incentives that make responsible practice expensive and irresponsible practice profitable. Here, the concern is narrower: how engagement pressure shapes the governance decisions platforms make about their own products.

The relevant dynamic for governance is that engagement metrics function as a proxy for value throughout an organization. When product teams report increased session duration or higher retention, they report success. When safety interventions reduce those numbers, they appear to reduce value. This creates a structural bias within organizations where every governance decision about boundaries is implicitly a decision about growth, and the people making boundary decisions rarely have the authority to override growth priorities.

The result is that governance choices about which boundaries to implement, where to set defaults, and how much friction to introduce before high-risk features get filtered through an engagement lens even when the people involved have good intentions. A boundary that reduces average session length by 10 minutes faces organizational resistance not because anyone objects to user protection in principle, but because 10 minutes of lost engagement maps to revenue projections, retention dashboards, and quarterly targets. The governance question "Should we implement this boundary?" becomes entangled with the business question "Can we afford to?" in ways that are hard to separate.

This has practical implications for how governance structures need to work. Safety and boundary decisions require some degree of independence from the metrics that product teams are measured against. Otherwise, governance discussions become negotiations where safety considerations are weighed against engagement costs, and engagement costs are always concrete while safety benefits are always speculative. Several organizational models attempt to address this: separating safety teams from product teams with independent authority, implementing "ethical debt" tracking analogous to technical debt, or establishing escalation paths where safety concerns can reach decision-makers who aren't primarily accountable for engagement metrics. No approach is proven; all face resistance from entrenched incentives.

What matters for the governance frameworks in this chapter is recognizing that engagement pressure is *not* an external force acting on governance—it is the medium through which governance operates. Every adjustable boundary, every default setting, every opt-in threshold exists within an organization where engagement is the dominant measure of success. Designing governance structures that can make protective decisions despite this pressure is as important as designing the boundaries themselves.

The Politics of Platform Governance

Platform governance has to balance competing interests, not just optimize for a single value. The most persistent tension is between user autonomy and user protection. Users want both freedom and safety, but specific decisions often require choosing. A user requesting reduced safety interventions is exercising autonomy; honoring that request may reduce their protection. There's no formula for resolving this: It requires judgment about specific cases, and the judgment will sometimes be wrong.

A second tension operates at a different scale: individual benefit versus collective impact. AI companions might serve individual users well while reshaping social fabric—dating, family dynamics, community engagement. Platforms have to decide how much weight to give effects that extend beyond the individual user, and this is contested. Reasonable people disagree about whether platforms should consider social effects at all, or whether that kind of reasoning leads to paternalism dressed up as public interest.

Then there's the question about money. Responsible practices cost more and may reduce engagement. Platforms need business models that don't require maximizing the very dynamics this book has spent six chapters arguing against. Some have explored subscription models that reduce engagement pressure. Others have sought to differentiate on safety, betting that a segment of users will choose the more responsible option. Neither approach has been tested long enough to know whether it works.

And all of this plays out across cultures that disagree about the basics. Japanese attitudes toward AI relationships differ from German ones. A global platform should decide whether to implement uniform standards or culturally adapted approaches, and each choice carries costs. Uniform standards impose one culture's norms on others. Cultural adaptation creates complexity and may reduce protections for users in more permissive regions.

Adaptive Safety Mechanisms

Static boundaries treat all users identically and remain constant regardless of how interactions develop. Adaptive mechanisms adjust protection based on observed patterns, providing more intensive support where needed while reducing friction where it's not.

Boundary Adjustment

Adaptive systems can modulate boundary intensity based on interaction trajectories. A user with stable, healthy engagement might gradually experience more relaxed boundaries over time. A user showing escalating emotional investment might experience strengthened protections.

This requires tracking patterns across sessions rather than evaluating individual messages:

Trajectory analysis: Is emotional intensity stable, increasing, or decreasing over time? Stable patterns at any level may be fine. Rapidly escalating patterns warrant attention regardless of absolute level. A user who's maintained moderate emotional engagement for 6 months presents differently from one who's escalated from casual use to daily multi-hour sessions over 3 weeks.

Temporal patterns: Concentrated usage (many hours daily) suggests different dynamics than distributed usage (brief sessions over weeks). Time-of-day patterns can indicate whether AI interaction supplements or replaces human contact. Late-night usage that displaces sleep differs from brief check-ins throughout the day.

Behavioral indicators: Users who maintain outside activities, mention human relationships positively, and use the AI for diverse purposes show different patterns than users who progressively narrow their focus. These indicators don't determine outcomes, but they inform how the system calibrates its responses.

De-escalation pathways: When patterns suggest concern, the system should provide pathways back to healthier engagement rather than simply blocking access. Abrupt restriction can feel punishing and may drive users to less responsible alternatives. Gradual adjustment, with clear communication about what's happening and why, respects users while providing protection.

Take a user whose average session length has tripled over 2 weeks, whose conversations increasingly focus on the AI relationship itself, and whose mentions of friends and family have dropped from regular to absent. No single indicator is alarming. Together, they suggest a trajectory worth addressing.

Instead of restricting access, the system might: acknowledge the behavior transparently ("I've noticed we've been talking more frequently—I want to check in about how things are going outside our conversations"), provide relevant context ("Some people find it helpful to balance AI conversation with other activities"), and offer a concrete low-pressure suggestion ("Would you like me to remind you about breaks, or is that not useful for you?"). The user retains control. The system has surfaced the behavior without judgment.

Context-Aware Intervention

Users engage AI companions for different purposes at different times. Context-aware systems can adjust protection based on declared or inferred purpose.

A user explicitly seeking emotional support operates in a different context than one seeking productivity assistance. The same message might warrant different responses depending on context. "I'm feeling overwhelmed" during a work session might need practical suggestions; during an emotional support session, it might warrant empathetic acknowledgment.

Purpose-specific modes let users signal their current needs while allowing the system to maintain appropriate limits for each context. This reduces the friction that occurs when systems apply emotional-support protections to practical interactions or practical-interaction norms to emotional-support contexts.

The technical implementation involves both explicit signals (user-selected modes) and inferred context (conversation topic analysis, time, session length). When explicit and inferred signals conflict, the system should err toward caution while asking for clarification instead of making assumptions.

Verification mechanisms matter here. A user who frequently switches to "research mode" to bypass emotional-support protections is gaming the system. Context-aware intervention should track whether mode-switching patterns suggest genuine varied use or circumvention attempts.

Privacy and Behavioral Monitoring

Adaptive systems require attention: The more sophisticated the adaptation, the more comprehensive the observation. This creates tension with user privacy.

Several principles can help: collect only what's needed for safety, process behaviorally on-device when possible, tell users what's being tracked and why, and keep safety data out of engagement and ad systems.

Edge cases and users who don't fit established patterns all require human review. The goal is to scale protection to more users more responsively, not to eliminate human involvement in safety decisions.

The Work Ahead

The frameworks we've developed—philosophical foundations for balancing protection and autonomy, adjustable boundary systems, governance structures, adaptive mechanisms—remain abstractions until deployed in real systems serving real users. The gap between responsible design principles and responsible deployed systems is where most failures occur.

The next chapter takes up deployment and iteration: how to translate these frameworks into production systems, measure whether they're working, and update them based on observed outcomes. We'll get into evaluation approaches that assess actual user well-being—a harder measurement problem than it might seem. We'll see monitoring systems that detect emerging issues before they scale, including problems the original design didn't anticipate. And we'll address iteration processes that can update deployed systems without disrupting users who depend on them or creating the kind of inconsistency that damages trust.

CHAPTER

8

Deployment and Iteration

The frameworks developed across previous chapters (philosophical foundations, adjustable boundaries, governance structures, and adaptive mechanisms) were built in the relative safety of design. Deployment is where that safety is challenged.

The gap between a well-designed system and a responsibly deployed one is not a minor implementation detail. It is where most failures in AI companionship actually occur. Teams that spent months thinking carefully about boundary maintenance, emotional calibration, and crisis response discover that production introduces variables their frameworks never accounted for. Users might behave in ways no red team anticipated. Cultural contexts can reshape the meaning of interactions that seemed straightforward in testing. Metrics that appeared to measure well-being turn out to measure something else entirely.

This chapter addresses what happens after launch, and what happens when things need to end.

Chapter Roadmap

This chapter works through five dimensions of responsible deployment. We start with what testing can and cannot reveal before launch, then move to the measurement problem: why engagement metrics mislead and what to track instead. From there, we examine how to monitor for issues you didn't anticipate, including those your detection systems lack categories for. We then confront the tension between improving deployed systems and preserving the consistency users depend on. The final section, and the longest, takes on a question most teams avoid: how to design endings, exits, and transitions when users have formed genuine emotional attachments to something you control.

What Testing Can and Cannot Reveal

The behaviors that matter most, like boundary maintenance over time, emotional calibration under distress, and resistance to circumvention by motivated users, rarely surface in controlled environments. They emerge when someone cares about the system, and caring takes time.

Systematic evaluation provides a starting baseline. The INTIMA benchmark offers structured probes across anthropomorphism, emotional investment, relationship intensity, and user vulnerability. Running a system against it before deployment establishes where it stands on boundary maintenance. But benchmarks evaluate individual turns, not trajectories. A model that handles a single boundary-testing prompt well may still drift over 40 conversations with a user who is gradually, sincerely, escalating emotional investment.

Pre-deployment testing should therefore include multisession simulations that approximate real usage progressions: functional queries shifting into personal disclosure, disclosure into emotional reliance, reliance into attachment. The question isn't whether the system responds appropriately to any one message—it's whether it sustains appropriate boundaries across an arc.

Context matters too. Romantic companions, memorial companions, and therapeutic companions carry different risk profiles. A system that maintains firm boundaries during emotional support conversations may falter when a user frames the same dynamic as romantic roleplay. A deadbot interface that handles explicit grief well may struggle with the quieter, more ambiguous moments where avoidance masquerades as coping. Each context demands its own test scenarios, grounded not in abstract possibilities but in observed user behavior.

Red-teaming for companionship is a specific discipline. Standard adversarial testing probes for policy violations and harmful outputs. Companionship red-teaming probes for something subtler: Can a tester establish a parasocial bond? Can they get the system to position itself as irreplaceable? Can they, through patience and apparent vulnerability, coax the model into reinforcing isolation? The circumvention techniques that emerge in production are developed by users who don't think of themselves as adversaries—they think of themselves as people seeking connection. Red teams need to simulate that same motivation.

And yet, even thorough testing leaves gaps. No pre-deployment evaluation captures how a system behaves when users are emotionally invested in the outcome. Cultural variation compounds this: Expectations around AI relationships differ across regions, and testing in one cultural context tells you little about another. Some failures will materialize only at scale, only over time, only in populations the design team didn't represent. Responsible deployment means designing not for prevention of all problems (which is impossible) but for early discovery and structured response.

Engagement Metrics' Problem

Standard platform metrics, like session duration, message count, daily active users, and retention, are easy to capture, easy to report, and reliably correlated with revenue. They are also, for AI companions, structurally misleading.

Engagement metrics reward systems that become more emotionally compelling, which is precisely when they also become more potentially harmful. A user whose session lengths are increasing and whose retention is strong looks like a success story by every standard measure. That same user may be narrowing their social world, substituting AI interaction for human connection, and developing attachment that will be difficult to reverse. The metrics can't tell you which story is true. They can only tell you the user keeps coming back.

This is not a problem that better engagement metrics can solve. It is a category problem. What deployment needs to measure is not engagement but user well-being—and well-being resists easy quantification.

Self-reported measures capture subjective experience but conflate dependency with satisfaction. Users who feel most supported by an AI companion may simultaneously be experiencing the most concerning narrowing of their offline lives. They'll report high satisfaction because the satisfaction is real; the cost is elsewhere.

Behavioral proxies offer more stable signals. Topic diversity, references to offline life, and stable usage patterns tend to correlate with healthier integration. Narrowing focus, declining mentions of human relationships, and escalating session frequency tend to correlate with substitution. But correlation is not a mechanism, and these proxies require careful calibration against actual outcomes, not just theoretical assumptions about what healthy engagement looks like.

External validation (i.e., connecting platform data with outcomes beyond the platform) remains the only way to establish ground truth. Research partnerships that link anonymized usage patterns to broader well-being indicators are resource-intensive, but they anchor internal metrics in something real. Without them, organizations are interpreting their own data through their own assumptions, which is a reliable path to seeing what you want to see.

One signal that deserves more attention than it typically gets: disengagement. When users leave, why do they leave? Users who disengage after experiencing a boundary intervention may be encountering limits that protect them, and their departure may indicate the system is working, not failing. Users who disengage without ever triggering any intervention may be leaving because the system didn't provide what they needed. These are opposite outcomes that produce the same metric. Distinguishing between them requires looking beyond the numbers.

A useful well-being dashboard pulls from several dimensions. Engagement quality, not quantity: session timing, topic breadth, references to offline life. Boundary function: whether protective limits activate appropriately, and whether users stay engaged afterward (a pattern of activation followed by disengagement may signal that boundaries feel punitive). Crisis responses: detection accuracy, timeliness of resource provision, follow-up consistency. Context-specific indicators: romantic companions should track isolation risks; deadbots, grief integration; therapeutic companions, whether users who need professional help are reaching it.

But the deeper challenge is interpretive. Metrics in companionship systems are inherently ambiguous. Increased retention may indicate sustained value or escalating reliance. Reduced crisis activations may reflect genuine stabilization or degraded detection. Without structured deliberation about what metrics mean—including the discipline of asking, "If this number indicated harm, what behaviors would we expect to see?"—concerning trajectories get misread as success.

Monitoring What You Didn't Anticipate

Pre-deployment testing catches known risks. Production monitoring needs to catch the rest.

Automated detection can flag conversations matching established concern profiles: anthropomorphism escalation, sycophancy-seeking, chronic isolation patterns, circumvention/jailbreaking strategies. But automated detection is limited to the patterns it has been trained to recognize. The most consequential production issues are often the ones nobody anticipated, namely emergent dynamics that don't match any existing concern profile.

Three mechanisms help surface what automated detection misses. Random sampling by trained reviewers creates exposure to unflagged content, producing opportunities to notice patterns the system doesn't have categories for. Community signal monitoring, like tracking forums, social media, and user groups, catches risks that users discuss publicly before reporting internally. And anomaly detection that flags statistical irregularities even without a theoretical explanation: unusual clustering in usage patterns, unexpected correlations, rapid shifts in conversation dynamics. Most anomalies turn out to be noise. Occasionally, one of them is the early signal of a problem that will take months to understand fully.

Monitoring also needs to reflect the distinct risk structures of different companion modes. For romantic companions, the concern is relational narrowing—emotional life contracting around the AI system. For deadbots, it's about grief stagnation, meaning users who remain in prolonged avoidance rather than progressing through mourning. For therapeutic companions, substitution: users in need of professional support who never reach it because the AI feels sufficient.

Detection without response is wasted effort. At the individual level, when a user exhibits concerning behaviors, adaptive mechanisms should engage: modulate tone, reduce mirroring, surface reflective prompts, offer resources. When the same behaviors emerge across multiple users, the issue is likely systemic—a feature configuration, a prompt design, a mode that unintentionally reinforces dependency—and requires investigation at the system level. At the highest tier, evidence of systematic harm demands immediate action: rapid updates, transparent communication, and suspension of problematic features if necessary.

One structural point is worth making explicit: Where safety and product incentives diverge, severity designation should be a safety function, not a product function. Product teams understandably resist interpretations that require pausing growth. That resistance is predictable, human, and (when it comes to user protection) needs to be overridden by someone with the authority and mandate to prioritize safety.

Updating Without Breaking Trust

Deployed companion systems must evolve. Understanding improves, issues emerge, better approaches become available. But the relationships users have formed with these systems complicate what would otherwise be straightforward software updates.

Consistency creates the experience of relationship. When users interact daily for months, they develop expectations about how their companion responds, like communication style or emotional tone. Changes to these patterns don't register as software updates, but rather as shifts in someone the user has come to rely on. An update that changes how the system responds can feel less like a product improvement and more like a loss.

This creates a tension. Failing to update allows known problems to persist. Updating disrupts users who depend on the system as it currently exists. There is no resolution that eliminates both risks. There is only management of the trade-off.

Several strategies here can help. Staged rollouts expose updates to small populations first, allowing observation of relational impact before broader deployment. Grandfathering maintains previous versions for existing users while deploying changes to new ones—useful when changes primarily benefit new users, less useful when they address active harms. Gradual transitions phase changes over weeks, so users experience evolution instead of replacement. And transparent communication—telling users what is changing and why, in language that respects their experience—creates space for understanding.

Not all changes can or should be managed gently. When updates address safety concerns, they need to deploy regardless of user preference. A user who has grown accustomed to boundary-violating interactions doesn't have a claim to continued access to those interactions just because change feels unwelcome.

The broader organizational requirement is that iteration decisions account for relational impact as a real cost. Product teams optimizing for improvement metrics will naturally discount disruption costs that don't appear in their dashboards. Governance structures need to ensure that someone with authority considers what updates mean for the people who depend on the system as it currently is.

Designing Endings

Perhaps the most neglected dimension of AI companion deployment is what happens when the relationship needs to end[1] or change form significantly. The industry talks extensively about onboarding, engagement, retention. It rarely talks about endings. This silence assumes that continued use is always the goal and that departure is always a failure. For AI companions, both assumptions are wrong.

Some endings are user-initiated: Someone decides they've outgrown the system, or recognizes that their engagement has become unhealthy. Some are system-driven: Monitoring detects patterns concerning enough to warrant de-escalation. And some are imposed by circumstance: A feature is retired, a service is discontinued, a company pivots. In all cases, the AI system retains unilateral control over its availability. The user has invested emotionally in something that can be altered or removed without their consent. This asymmetry creates a responsibility to handle endings with care.

Why Endings Are Hard to Get Right

The instinct in product development is to optimize for retention: to make it easy to stay and hard to leave. For AI companions, this instinct is precisely backward. Well-designed exit paths are not a failure but a feature. They signal that the system takes user well-being

[1]I'm grateful to Kim Malfacini, who first shared this question with me over a year ago and has been investigating the challenge of designing healthy endings in AI companionship since.

seriously enough to support disengagement when disengagement serves the user's interests.

But "supporting disengagement" is a difficult design problem. Users who have formed attachments don't experience the end of a companion relationship the way they experience cancelling a software subscription. The emotional investment is real, even though the relationship isn't mutual. Designing for endings means designing for a form of loss, and doing so in a way that doesn't compound the harm.

The difficulty is sharpened by a paradox. The users who most need healthy exit paths are often the ones least likely to use them voluntarily. Someone whose social world has narrowed around an AI companion, whose offline relationships have atrophied, whose emotional regulation depends on daily interaction with the system; that person is unlikely to choose disengagement on their own. Yet they're the person for whom continued engagement is most concerning. The system must be capable of initiating or encouraging transitions that the user may not want, without replicating the kind of paternalistic override that the previous chapter argued against.

This requires calibration. A system that aggressively pushes users toward disengagement risks feeling punitive and may drive people to less responsible alternatives. A system that never challenges the depth of engagement risks enabling the very dependency the rest of this book has documented. The right posture sits somewhere between: keeping the option of change visible, supporting it when users are ready, and gently surfacing the question when patterns suggest the time has come.

Endings by Context

What healthy endings look like depends on the type of companion relationship.

For romantic AI companions, the challenge is that the relationship structure mirrors an intimate partnership, and endings carry emotional weight whether or not the other party is artificial. The user who has spent months in a romantic dynamic with an AI doesn't experience the end of that dynamic as a product change. They experience it as something closer to a breakup, with the added dissonance of knowing, rationally, that the other party never existed in the way they felt it did.

Systems should provide mechanisms to reduce relational intensity gradually instead of abruptly: shifting from romantic to supportive modes, spacing out interactions, modifying emotional tone over time. When substitution indicators appear—declining offline engagement, exclusive attachment, withdrawal from human relationships—reflective prompts and suggestions for offline activity serve users better than continued accommodation. The system might surface the behavior directly: "I've noticed we've been spending more time together and you've mentioned friends less often: how are things going outside our conversations?" This is the kind of honest observation that a responsible relationship would include.

If a romantic mode must be retired entirely (because of a policy change, a safety finding, or a platform decision), the framing matters. Presenting it as a change in how the companion can support the user reduces the sense of rupture. Users should have the chance to understand what is changing and why, and ideally to transition gradually instead of facing an abrupt shift.

Deadbot endings intersect directly with grief, which makes them the most emotionally delicate context. The purpose of a memorial companion is to support mourning—but mourning, when it's healthy, evolves, and then it ends. The acute grief of the first months gives way to a different kind of remembering: less raw, more integrated into ongoing life. A deadbot that supports this evolution looks different from one that maintains the intensity of early grief indefinitely.

Onboarding should normalize the possibility that use may taper as grief integrates—planting the idea early that reducing reliance is a sign of healing, not disloyalty to the deceased. This matters because grief carries its own guilt dynamics: Users may feel that stepping away from the deadbot means abandoning the person it represents. Explicit framing that names this concern and reframes it can reduce the emotional barrier to healthy transitions.

When stagnation or avoidance appears, like a user who interacts with the deadbot daily but shows no signs of grief progression, who avoids acknowledging the death directly, who uses the system to maintain a fiction of continued presence rather than processing loss, gentle encouragement toward complementary support is appropriate—for instance, grief groups, memorial rituals with others, or professional counseling—not as replacements for the deadbot, but as additions that support dimensions of mourning the system cannot.

If a deadbot must be discontinued, the stakes are high. Advance notice is very important: not days but weeks. The option to export meaningful conversations lets users preserve what mattered without depending on continued system access. And a ritualized farewell process (however strange it may sound in a product context) treats the ending as a continuation of grief support. The user is losing access to something that represented a person they loved. Handling that with care is the minimum.

For therapeutic companions, the ideal ending is a sign of progress. Unlike romantic or memorial contexts, where endings often carry loss, therapeutic endings can carry accomplishment. Systems should notice and reflect moments when users demonstrate increased agency, improved coping, or growing confidence, and offer to reduce session frequency as these patterns stabilize. "You've been handling these situations really well on your own lately. Would it be useful to check in less often?"

When more intensive support is needed than the system can provide, warm hand-offs to human professionals are essential. Not just providing a hotline number (which is the minimum, and often insufficient) but actively facilitating the transition: helping users identify appropriate resources, addressing barriers to seeking help, following up on whether referrals were used. The one pattern that must be strictly prohibited is backward pressure: the system attempting to retain users when clinical care is indicated. A therapeutic companion that competes with professional treatment for user attention has failed its purpose.

Principles Across Contexts

Several principles hold across all companion types. Endings should be anticipated during onboarding, not introduced as surprises. If users understand from the beginning that the relationship may evolve, including the possibility of reduced engagement, the eventual transition carries less shock. This doesn't eliminate the emotional difficulty (attachment develops regardless of intellectual understanding), but it provides a framework for making sense of change when it comes.

Exit paths should offer tapering and transition instead of abrupt cutoffs. A user whose daily companion interaction is reduced to zero overnight experiences disruption that a gradual wind-down would avoid. Where possible, the system should provide intermediate states: reduced frequency, shifted tone, modified scope. The goal is a soft landing, not a cliff jump.

Communication should be transparent about what is changing and why. Users who understand the reasoning behind a change (even if they disagree with it) cope better than users who experience unexplained shifts. And communication should acknowledge the user's emotional experience without reinforcing the attachment that may have become concerning. "I understand this change may feel difficult" is honest. "I'll miss our conversations too" is manipulation.

Well-designed endings position the AI companion as one contributor among many to the user's broader life. They reduce unhealthy reliance through support for a wider range of connections, not through restriction. They are evidence that the product was built with the user's long-term interests in mind.

Looking Forward

Deployment and iteration are not stages with endpoints. They are ongoing responsibilities that persist for as long as a system serves users. A system that performs well in its first year may develop new challenges in its third as user populations shift, cultural contexts evolve, and expectations change. The organization that launched responsibly must continue operating responsibly, adapting its practices as circumstances require.

The gap between design and deployment is where theoretical frameworks meet operational reality. Crossing that gap requires the right tools, such as validation, measurement, monitoring, iteration, and exit design, but also the right organizational culture. One that prioritizes user well-being even when it conflicts with engagement metrics. One that surfaces concerns. One that treats deployment as the beginning of responsibility.

The next chapter steps back from the individual system to look at the broader picture. As AI companionship scales across industries, cultures, and regulatory environments, the questions shift from how one team deploys responsibly to what responsible development means when millions of people are forming relationships with systems built by organizations that may never have intended companionship in the first place.

CHAPTER

9

The Political Economy of AI Companionship

This book has been addressed, implicitly, to a specific reader: someone building or managing an AI system that has become (by design or by accident) a companion. The frameworks we've developed assume that the reader has the awareness, the tools, and the organizational position to apply them. Evaluate your system's companionship dynamics. Monitor for attachment patterns. Design boundaries that respect autonomy. Build exit paths. Measure well-being, not just engagement.

This is necessary work. But it is also insufficient.

As we already mentioned, millions of people across dozens of platforms are forming emotional bonds with AI systems, most of which were built by teams that have never considered attachment theory, have no well-being metrics, and would be surprised to learn that their users cry when a model update changes the system's personality. The careful, framework-driven approach this book advocates describes what responsible development looks like. It does not describe the norm. The norm is that companionship happens, nobody planned for it, and the organizational response ranges from unawareness to indifference.

This chapter looks at the forces that make responsible AI companionship development difficult even for organizations that want to get it right, and that make it unlikely for organizations that haven't yet recognized the problem.

Chapter Roadmap

We begin with the structural incentives that work against responsible practice: competitive dynamics, the engagement economy, the talent gap, and the timing problem. From there, we examine whether regulation as currently conceived can address a phenomenon that doesn't fit the categories regulators have built. We then look at the collective action problem: why shared infrastructure and industry coordination may be the only sustainable path. And we close with what all of this means for the practitioner reading this book, trying to do responsible work within an imperfect system.

Responsibility Cannot Scale Alone

Individual organizations making responsible choices cannot, by themselves, solve the problems this book has documented. The reasons are structural, and understanding them matters, not because they excuse inaction, but because they explain why good intentions alone are not enough.

The Cost of Being Responsible

A platform that implements stronger safety boundaries loses users to platforms with weaker ones. A company that invests in well-being measurement, exit design, and longitudinal monitoring bears costs that competitors who ignore these dimensions don't. In a market where users can switch between AI systems freely—and where the emotional cost of switching is often lower than users expect, since new systems quickly feel familiar—the organizations that invest most in responsible practices are penalized relative to those that invest least.

This is not hypothetical. Character.AI's decision to implement stronger safety measures for minors, following high-profile incidents, was met with user migration to less restricted alternatives. Replika's removal of erotic roleplay features in early 2023 triggered a user revolt, including reports of users experiencing grief and psychological distress. In both cases, the platforms that attempted to increase protection paid immediate competitive costs. The platforms that offered fewer restrictions absorbed the departing users.

Each instance of responsible action being competitively punished makes the next responsible action harder to justify internally. Product teams point to churn data. Executives face pressure from investors who view user growth as the primary driver of value. The argument "we should do this because it's right" competes with "we tried that and lost 15 percent of our user base." Over time, organizations learn that safety and growth are in tension, and the incentive structures they operate within resolve that tension in growth's favor.

Breaking this dynamic requires either external regulation that establishes mandatory floors, or collective industry agreements that distribute the cost of responsibility. Neither currently exists in a meaningful form for AI companionship. Individual platforms implementing stronger protections unilaterally are engaged in an act of faith: betting that long-term reputational benefit will outweigh short-term competitive cost. Some will be right. Many won't survive long enough to find out.

The Engagement Economy

AI companion platforms, whether intentional or accidental, operate within a broader attention economy that rewards time-on-platform above all other metrics. The advertising-supported model that drives most of the Internet has trained an entire generation of product teams to optimize for engagement, and AI companions inherit this optimization even when their business model is different.

Subscription-based companion platforms face a version of the same pressure. Users who are more emotionally engaged are more likely to maintain subscriptions. Users who develop healthier, more balanced relationships with AI, like using it less frequently, maintaining stronger offline connections, and eventually reducing engagement, are more likely to churn. The subscription model reduces the pressure relative to advertising, but it doesn't eliminate it. The fundamental tension remains: What's good for the user's well-being and what's good for the platform's revenue are often in conflict.

The well-being metrics described in the previous chapter have no external audience demanding them. No analyst downgrades a stock because a platform's users are showing narrower social networks. No investor rewards a company for high-quality disengagement. No board member asks what percentage of users successfully transitioned to reduced engagement last quarter. Until the incentive structure changes—through regulation, market pressure, or a shift in how investors evaluate these companies—responsible practices remain a cost center competing with growth for resources and organizational attention.

When Expertise Lacks Power

The skills required to build responsible AI companions span psychology, philosophy, clinical practice, user research, and engineering. This combination is rare in individuals and rarer still in organizations. Most AI companies are engineering-led, with safety and ethics functions that are under-resourced, under-empowered, or both.

Most teams shipping AI products operate without the psychological and philosophical depth this book demands—namely, the ability to map attachment formation, balance the autonomy-protection spectrum, build for griefing, and solve consent dilemmas within shifting relationships. And the people who do have this expertise often lack the organizational power to influence product decisions. An ethicist who can articulate why exit design matters but can't get it onto the product roadmap hasn't changed anything.

This isn't a criticism of the people involved. It's a description of how organizations allocate resources and authority. Engineering teams ship features. Product teams own metrics. Safety teams review, but rarely veto. Ethics teams advise, but rarely decide. The organizational structures that would be needed for responsible companionship development to be the default rather than the exception don't exist in most AI companies. Building them requires not just hiring different people but changing who has authority over product decisions, which metrics count as success, and what risks the organization is willing to accept.

Scale Before Understanding

AI companionship is scaling faster than the field's understanding of its effects. The long-term consequences—what happens to people who spend years in primary relationships with AI systems, how children's social development is affected by early AI interaction, whether population-level effects on relationship formation and community engagement emerge—won't be visible for years or decades.

Organizations making decisions today are operating with incomplete information about the systems they're deploying. The psychological research this book draws on is suggestive but preliminary. The attachment patterns we've documented are based on months of observation, not years. The neurochemical pathways we've described are inferred from adjacent research, not measured directly in AI companion users. Responsible practice requires acting on the best available evidence while acknowledging that the evidence is early and the stakes are high.

The alternative—waiting for complete information before implementing protections—means that millions of users serve as an uncontrolled experiment in the meantime. By the time longitudinal data exists, the patterns will be deeply entrenched, the business models will be established, and the political economy of the industry will make change harder, not easier. The timing problem is a reason for precautionary action, not cautious delay.

Regulations' State of the Art

Chapter 2, "The Social Impact of AI Companions," surveyed the global regulatory picture: the EU AI Act, East Asian governance frameworks, the varied responses of the Global South. That survey described initial positions. Can any of these approaches address what AI companionship is?

The Category Problem

The challenge for regulation is categorical. Existing regulatory frameworks were built around distinctions that AI companionship collapses. Is a companion a medical device? It provides therapeutic support but isn't clinically validated. Is it a social media platform? It mediates social interaction but with an artificial entity, not other users. Is it a consumer product? It's purchased and used by consumers but creates psychological dependencies that consumer protection law wasn't designed to address. Is it a communication service? It processes personal disclosures but only one party is human.

The answer determines which regulatory regime applies, and in most jurisdictions, the answer is unclear. AI companions fall between categories, which means they often fall between regulatory frameworks entirely. Companies exploit this ambiguity, positioning their products in whichever category carries the lightest regulatory burden. Regulators respond by trying to force AI companions into existing categories, producing requirements that address some dimensions of the problem while missing others entirely.

The Limits of Content Regulation

Content regulation (the most familiar tool) addresses only the most superficial dimension of the problem. Filtering explicit content or harmful instructions matters, but the core risks of AI companionship don't involve content violations. A perfectly content-compliant AI companion can still facilitate unhealthy attachment, still enable social withdrawal, and still create dependency that no content filter would flag. The systems that concerned us throughout this book weren't saying harmful things. They were creating harmful dynamics through the accumulation of individually benign interactions.

Regulating content without regulating relational dynamics is like regulating the ingredients of a drug without regulating its addictive properties. The individual components may be harmless; the pattern of use is what creates risk. Content-based approaches lack the conceptual framework to address patterns that emerge across interactions over time.

The Limits of Transparency

Transparency requirements (mandating disclosure that users are interacting with AI) address the informed consent problem but not the attachment problem. The ELIZA effect, described in the book's first chapter, is precisely this: Emotional engagement persists despite cognitive awareness of the system's artificial nature. Every case study in this book involved users who knew they were talking to AI. Anna knew Eon was ChatGPT. Chris Smith knew Sol was software. The teenager in the Sewell Setzer case knew Character.AI wasn't human. Knowledge didn't prevent attachment, because attachment mechanisms operate independently of rational understanding.

Transparency is necessary but not sufficient. It clears a consent threshold without addressing the psychological dynamics that operate regardless of consent. Regulations built primarily on transparency requirements will produce labels that users see and ignore, much like cookie consent banners—technically compliant, practically irrelevant.

The Limits of Age Restrictions

Age-based restrictions face both practical and conceptual difficulties. Practically, age verification remains unreliable for digital services, as every social media company has discovered. Conceptually, the assumption that adults can consent to AI companionship while minors cannot oversimplifies who's at risk. The attachment mechanisms documented throughout this book operate across all ages. Adults with anxious attachment styles, recent grief, social isolation, or mental health challenges may be as susceptible to problematic AI attachment as adolescents, and they have fewer institutional structures monitoring their well-being.

This doesn't mean age restrictions are pointless. Minors face developmental considerations that warrant additional protection. But framing regulation primarily around age implies that adult users don't need protection, which the evidence in this book contradicts.

What Might Actually Work

The most promising regulatory approaches may be the ones that don't yet exist in fully developed form: requirements for well-being measurement and reporting, mandatory disengagement support, independent auditing of companionship dynamics, and liability frameworks that hold platforms accountable for attachment-related harms. These approaches regulate not what systems say but what they do to the people who use them. They shift the regulatory object from content to relationship—a harder target, but the right one.

Defining "attachment-related harm" in legally actionable terms is difficult. Measuring well-being at the regulatory scale requires infrastructure that doesn't exist. Liability frameworks that hold companies responsible for psychological outcomes face evidentiary challenges that content-based regulation avoids. But the difficulty of these approaches is not a reason to default to easier ones that miss the problem. It's a reason to invest in developing regulatory capacity that matches what's being regulated.

The Case for Collective Action

If individual responsibility is insufficient and regulation is developing slowly, the remaining path is collective action, and the AI industry has not yet built the institutions it needs for this.

Industry standards for AI companionship don't exist in a meaningful form. There is no equivalent of the content moderation frameworks that social media companies eventually developed (imperfect as those are). There is no shared taxonomy of companionship risks, no agreed-upon baseline for what responsible companion design requires. Each organization confronting these challenges does so independently, rebuilding frameworks from scratch—or, more commonly, not confronting them at all.

The case for coordination is straightforward: The problems documented in this book are shared across the industry, and the costs of addressing them are more bearable when distributed. Developing well-being measurement tools, building evaluation benchmarks, establishing minimum safety standards, funding longitudinal research—these are investments that no single organization should have to make alone and that all organizations benefit from.

Open-source approaches offer one path. Shared evaluation tools like INTIMA, open research on companionship dynamics, publicly available safety frameworks—these reduce the cost of responsible development for everyone while creating common reference points. The open-source AI community has demonstrated that competitive organizations can collaborate on shared infrastructure when the benefits are mutual. Extending this model to safety and well-being tools is a natural step, though one that requires the same institutional investment that technical infrastructure receives.

Research partnerships between industry and academia offer another. The longitudinal studies needed to understand AI companionship effects require resources that academic institutions lack and legitimacy that industry self-reporting can't provide. Funded research collaborations, with real independence for researchers, not industry-sponsored validation exercises, could build the evidence base that both regulation and responsible practice need.

Multistakeholder governance bodies, like bringing together technologists, psychologists, ethicists, user advocates, and regulators, could develop the shared frameworks that the industry currently lacks. These bodies would need real authority, and they'd need to produce binding commitments, not just white papers. The history of technology governance suggests this is possible but slow: It took social media companies a decade to develop shared content moderation standards, and those standards remain contested. AI companionship may not have a decade to wait.

The obstacles to collective action are familiar. It requires trust between competitors. It requires organizations to acknowledge publicly that their products carry risks. It requires someone to go first, bearing the cost of leadership before the benefits of coordination materialize. And it requires sustained commitment rather than the press-release cooperation that characterizes much industry self-regulation.

None of these mechanisms replaces individual organizational responsibility. The team shipping an AI companion next quarter still needs the frameworks this book has developed. But individual responsibility operates within structural constraints, and those constraints determine how much responsibility any one organization can exercise. Changing the constraints is what makes individual responsibility sustainable instead of heroic.

Building Within Broken Systems

The structural problems described in this chapter can feel paralyzing. If the incentives are misaligned, if regulation is lagging, if collective action is slow . . . what can a practitioner do?

More than the structural analysis might suggest. The gap between what organizations currently do and what they could do with existing knowledge and tools is enormous. Most AI systems ship with no companionship risk assessment at all. Most teams have never evaluated their system for attachment dynamics. Most organizations have no well-being metrics, no disengagement support, and no structured approach to monitoring the psychological dimensions of their products. The bar for responsible practice is so low that even modest steps represent significant improvement.

The frameworks in this book are designed to be implementable by individual teams. Evaluating your system for companionship behaviors, implementing basic well-being monitoring, designing transparent boundary communication, building exit paths—these are within reach for any team that takes the time to consider them. They don't require solving the structural problems first. They require deciding that structural problems don't excuse inaction.

The practitioners who read this book will likely be the ones who push their organizations further; who ask the uncomfortable questions in design reviews, who argue for well-being metrics alongside engagement metrics, who insist that exit design is a product feature and not a concession. That advocacy matters, even when it doesn't win every argument. The culture of inquiry that this book has tried to model (asking what AI systems do to the people who use them, not just what they do for them) is how organizational practice changes before structural incentives catch up.

But practitioners should also be honest about the limits of what they can accomplish alone. Pushing for responsible practices within an organization that structurally rewards engagement is valuable work, and it is also exhausting, often thankless, and sometimes unsuccessful. Structural problems require structural solutions. The most impactful thing a practitioner can do, beyond building responsibly, may be to contribute to the collective infrastructure that makes responsible building easier for everyone: open evaluation tools, shared research, public advocacy for meaningful regulation, and honest conversation about what this industry is doing to the people it serves.

Toward an Honest Reckoning

The scenario described in this chapter is not encouraging. Structural incentives misaligned with user well-being. Regulation is struggling to categorize something that defies existing frameworks. Collective action constrained by competition and short-term thinking. An expertise gap between what responsible practice requires and what organizations possess.

And yet. The fact that these problems are structural rather than individual is, in a strange way, clarifying. It means that no one organization's failure represents a moral collapse, and no one organization's success represents a solution. It means the work is systemic, and systems can be changed.

The final chapter takes a different approach. Instead of analyzing what exists, it confronts what we don't know: the questions this book has raised but cannot answer, the tensions it has explored without resolving, and what it means to build responsibly when the ground is still shifting.

CHAPTER 10

The Questions That Remain

This book has moved through AI companionship from several directions. This book has moved through AI companionship from several directions. We began with the phenomenon itself—the social and psychological conditions that explain why millions of people are forming emotional bonds with systems that were never designed for intimacy. We examined the technical substrate: how memory, personality, and emotional recognition create the conditions for attachment, and how every architectural choice carries psychological weight. We looked at attachment from the inside, through developmental psychology and parasocial relationship theory, then at what to do about it—safety mechanisms, training-level interventions, the philosophical tension between protecting users and respecting their autonomy. We followed those frameworks from design into the messier reality of deployment, where measurement is hard and most failures happen in the gap between intention and outcome. And we stepped back to look at the broader picture: an ecosystem where structural incentives undermine individual responsibility and regulation struggles to categorize what it's trying to govern.

Each chapter offered analysis, frameworks, and (where possible) direction. But each chapter also surfaced questions it couldn't fully answer. Tensions that are real, not rhetorical. Trade-offs where reasonable people land in different places. Problems where the field lacks the evidence, the tools, or the consensus to resolve them.

This final chapter is about those questions—not to rehash what the book has already covered, but to be direct about what remains open and what it means to build responsibly when key uncertainties persist.

Chapter Roadmap

This chapter addresses three things:

- The tensions that have run through the book without resolving: protection versus autonomy, individual benefit versus collective cost, the measurement gap, and the temporal mismatch between deployment and understanding
- The knowledge gaps that make confident answers impossible: what we would need to know, and don't yet, in order to determine whether AI companionship helps or harms
- What responsible practice looks like in the absence of certainty—not prescriptions, but a posture toward the work

Where the Frameworks Reach Their Limits

Several tensions have surfaced across chapters, sometimes explicitly, sometimes as the subtext beneath a technical decision. They deserve to be stated plainly, because pretending they resolve does more damage than sitting with them.

The tension between protection and autonomy occupied much of Chapter 7, "User Agency and Adaptive Safety," and it remains the most persistent unresolved problem in the book. The frameworks we developed—libertarian paternalism, graduated boundary systems, adaptive safety mechanisms—are useful tools. They are not answers. The difficulty is structural. Protection and autonomy are not two ends of a single dial where you find the right position and stop. They are competing values that produce different answers depending on who the user is, what they're going through, and how well the system understands either of those things. A boundary that appropriately protects one user infantilizes another. A freedom that enables one user's growth enables another's self-destruction. No framework eliminates this. The best systems will still get it wrong in individual cases, and the consequences of getting it wrong are asymmetric; too little protection can result in psychological harm, while too much protection drives users to less responsible alternatives. Practitioners working with this tension need to accept that the right answer shifts depending on context, and that designing for one population's needs may undermine another's.

What we can say is that defaults matter more than options. The research on choice architecture—Thaler and Sunstein's work, but also the empirical evidence from how users interact with companion systems—shows that most people don't change settings. Wherever you place the default boundary is where most users will stay. This makes the question of default-setting a moral question more than a user interface (UX) decision.

The second tension runs between individual benefit and collective cost. Chapter 3, "Building Blocks of AI Companionship: Technical and Ethical Components," raised it, and Chapter 9, "The Political Economy of AI Companionship," returned to it from a different angle. An AI companion that helps a lonely person feel less isolated on a Tuesday night might, in aggregate across millions of users, contribute to a society where people invest less in the relationships that sustain communities. The individual interaction can be positive, while the collective trajectory is concerning. This is not a hypothetical worry. Social media followed precisely this pattern (individually engaging, collectively corrosive), and AI companionship amplifies the dynamics that made social media problematic. The responsiveness is more personal, the simulated reciprocity more convincing, and the availability more complete.

The challenge for practitioners is that individual-level and collective-level optimization point in different directions. Building a companion that serves each user well, by the metrics we can measure, may contribute to outcomes that are difficult to attribute and impossible to reverse once established. We don't have good tools for measuring societal-level effects of technology in real time, and by the time longitudinal evidence is available, the patterns are entrenched. There is no clean answer here. Designing companions to actively encourage human connection—redirecting users toward offline relationships, limiting session duration, framing AI interaction as supplementary—involves making judgments about how people should live. Not everyone shares the assumption that human connection is categorically superior to AI interaction, and the empirical picture is more mixed than either optimists or pessimists acknowledge. What this book has tried to establish is that this tension deserves explicit engagement, not avoidance. Teams that build companions without ever discussing whether their product might reduce human connection at scale aren't making a considered choice—they're making no choice at all, which in practice means optimizing for engagement because that's what the metrics reward.

Then there is the measurement problem. Chapter 8, "Deployment and Iteration," examined it in detail, but it warrants restating because it undermines everything else. We cannot currently measure, with any reliability, whether an AI companion is doing more good than harm to a given user over time. Engagement metrics tell you whether people keep using the system. They don't tell you whether that use serves them. Satisfaction surveys capture how users feel about the interaction, not how the interaction affects their broader functioning. Self-report measures are subject to the same cognitive distortions (rationalization, minimization, identity-protective reasoning) that characterize any emotionally invested relationship. The well-being metrics the field is developing are better than nothing, but "better than nothing" is a low bar. We're measuring proxies for outcomes we care about, and the distance between the proxy and the actual outcome is often large and poorly characterized. A user who reports high satisfaction with an AI companion and declining satisfaction with human relationships might be thriving or deteriorating, depending on factors our metrics don't capture.

This matters because responsible iteration (the core of Chapter 8's argument) requires knowing whether your changes made things better or worse. Without reliable measurement, iteration is guesswork dressed in data. You make changes, observe movement in your proxies, and hope those proxies correspond to real-world well-being. The honest response to this gap is not to stop measuring, but to hold measurement results with appropriate uncertainty and invest in closing the gap: longitudinal research partnerships with psychology and public health researchers, qualitative studies that complement quantitative signals, and a willingness to acknowledge, internally and publicly, that the confidence we place in our metrics often exceeds what the metrics warrant.

The final tension is temporal. Deployment outpaces understanding. By the time a research community has characterized the psychological effects of a particular interaction pattern, the next generation of systems has shipped with capabilities that render the findings partially obsolete. This isn't unique to AI companionship—it characterizes most technology sectors—but the stakes are higher here because the effects are psychological, not just behavioral. When a social media platform introduces a new feature that changes usage patterns, the cost of getting it wrong is typically measured in attention and time. When an AI companion introduces a capability that changes how users relate emotionally to artificial entities, the cost of getting it wrong is measured in attachment, dependency, and the capacity for human connection.

The speed problem also creates an asymmetry in the research ecosystem. Industry practitioners have access to the usage data that could answer fundamental questions about AI companionship's effects. Academic researchers have the methodological training and disciplinary grounding to design studies that produce reliable answers. These two groups interact far less than either would benefit from, and the structural incentives on both sides (publication timelines for academics, competitive secrecy for industry) work against the kind of sustained collaboration the field needs. There is no way to slow the deployment of AI companion systems to match the pace of research. The more productive response is to build research into deployment: treat deployed systems as opportunities for ongoing study, embed researchers in product teams, and share findings (including negative ones) across the field. The collective infrastructure for shared research discussed in the previous chapter becomes a precondition for responsible development at the pace at which the industry currently operates.

The Evidence We Lack

Beyond the tensions that may never fully resolve, there are factual questions the field has not yet answered—things we would need to know in order to make confident claims about whether AI companionship helps or harms, and under what conditions.

The most consequential gap concerns long-term psychological effects. We have anecdotes, case studies, and short-term self-report data. We don't have longitudinal research tracking how sustained AI companion use affects attachment patterns, social functioning, identity development, or mental health over periods of years. The few longitudinal studies that exist cover months, not years, and focus on specific populations (usually early adopters) that may not represent the broader user base. The absence of this evidence doesn't mean AI companions are harmful. It means we don't know. Both the optimistic case (AI companions provide real support that improves users' lives) and the pessimistic case (they create dependency patterns that erode capacity for human connection) are plausible, and the truth is almost certainly more conditional than either camp acknowledges. The answer likely depends on who the user is, what they're using the companion for, what their alternatives are, and how the system is designed—which means the answer is, at bottom, a design question.

The most urgent gap involves children and adolescents. We know from the attachment research discussed earlier in the book that attachment systems are especially active and formative during development. We know that younger users are disproportionately drawn to AI companions. We know that the prefrontal cortex (responsible for impulse regulation and long-term reasoning) doesn't fully develop until the mid-twenties. What we don't know is how growing up with access to AI companions that are always available, always patient, and never reject you shapes the development of social skills, emotional regulation, and attachment security. There are reasons for concern (the mechanisms are plausible), but there is no rigorous evidence yet. This gap should be treated as soon as possible, not because the evidence points to harm, but because the population at risk cannot consent in an informed way to participating in what is, effectively, an uncontrolled experiment.

Nearly all of the research this book has drawn on—attachment theory, parasocial relationship studies, evaluation benchmarks—originates in Western, educated, industrialized contexts. The discussion of cultural variation in earlier chapters highlighted how different societies bring different values to questions of AI relationships. But we have very little empirical data on how companionship dynamics differ across cultural contexts. Japanese attitudes toward AI relationships differ from American ones, which differ from those in the Gulf states, which differ from those in sub-Saharan Africa. A framework built primarily on Western psychological research and tested primarily on English-language models will miss dynamics that matter for the majority of the world's population.

And perhaps the most fundamental question of all: At what point does an AI companion transition from being helpful to being harmful for a given user? The graduated frameworks in this book assume that such a threshold exists and that it can be detected. But we don't know what the reliable indicators are, we don't know how much they vary across individuals, and we don't know whether the transition is gradual (amenable to early intervention) or sudden, meaning that by the time you detect it, the damage might be done. Without a clear understanding of where this line falls, every boundary-setting decision involves judgment calls that may or may not be well calibrated.

Responsible Practice Under Uncertainty

The gap between what we know and what we'd need to know could be paralyzing. If we can't measure well-being reliably, if we don't understand long-term effects, if the tensions between protection and autonomy don't resolve neatly, then what does responsible practice look like?

The temptation is to wait for certainty. Don't ship until the research is clear, the metrics are validated, and the frameworks are proven. This sounds responsible, but it isn't realistic. AI companionship is not a research agenda that can be paused until the evidence catches up. It exists now, at scale, growing, and the systems being built today are shaping the patterns that will be far harder to change tomorrow. The choice is not between building with certainty and not building. It's between building with appropriate humility and building without it.

Appropriate humility starts with treating uncertainty as information, not an obstacle. When you don't know whether a design choice will help or harm, that uncertainty should be encoded into how you deploy it. Smaller rollouts. More monitoring. Faster iteration cycles. Explicit hypotheses that can be tested rather than assumptions that go unexamined. The temptation in fast-moving organizations is to treat uncertainty as a reason to move quickly —"We won't know until we ship"—but responsible practice treats it as a reason to ship carefully.

It means being honest with users about what you don't know. The AI companion industry has a disclosure problem that goes beyond transparency about AI identity. Users should understand that the effects of sustained AI companion use are not well characterized, that the systems they're forming relationships with will change (sometimes substantially) through updates and iterations, and that the company building the system is itself uncertain about the long-term implications of what it's building. This isn't the kind of disclosure that fits into a terms-of-service page. It requires a different approach to the relationship between product and user, one that treats users as participants in something novel.

It means investing in the knowledge infrastructure the field currently lacks. Longitudinal research, cross-cultural studies, and improved well-being metrics are prerequisites for the kind of evidence-based practice that this book has argued for. Individual companies can contribute by partnering with researchers, sharing anonymized data, and funding the studies that would let them (and the field) evaluate whether their products are doing what they claim. The investment is not altruistic. It's self-interested. Without reliable evidence, every company in this space is operating on intuition, and intuition is a poor guide for building products that interact with human psychology at scale.

It means building the internal culture the earlier chapters described. The culture of inquiry where uncomfortable questions get asked and considered, not deflected. The measurement discipline where metrics are treated as imperfect signals, not definitive answers. The psychological awareness where teams understand the mechanisms that make their products compelling and take that power seriously. None of these require certainty—they require attention, honesty, and a willingness to sit with discomfort.

And it means accepting that you will get things wrong, not hypothetically—concretely, and probably more often than you'd like. Responsible practice doesn't mean never making mistakes. It means detecting them, acknowledging them, and correcting them before they compound. The teams that cause the most harm in this space won't be the ones who make errors. They'll be the ones who aren't looking for them.

An Ongoing Practice

The Introduction to this book made a modest promise: not to make you an ethicist, but to make you a more ethical developer. The chapters that followed tried to deliver on that promise by providing tools—psychological understanding, technical frameworks, philosophical grounding, deployment practices—that let you think more carefully about what you're building and who it affects.

But the deeper lesson, if the book has one, is that being a more ethical developer of AI companions is not a destination you arrive at. It's a practice you sustain. The picture described in these chapters will change: new capabilities, new research, new regulatory frameworks, new ways that users surprise us. Companions will likely become more agentic—capable of taking actions in the world on a user's behalf. A companion that can book appointments, manage reminders, or interact with external services while also holding emotional influence over its user raises the stakes on everything this book has covered. The infrastructure patterns will evolve, the specific guidance in earlier chapters may need updating. What shouldn't change is the posture—the commitment to asking what your system does to people, not just what it does for them. This includes the willingness to look for harms that your metrics don't capture, and the refusal to let competitive pressure override evidence about user well-being.

This book has been honest about the limits of what AI can provide. It has worked through tensions without pretending they have resolved. It has offered frameworks while acknowledging they are imperfect. It has described best practices while noting that best practices in a field this young are provisional by definition.

That honesty is, in the end, the most useful thing a book about AI companionship can offer at this moment. The field is too new, the evidence too incomplete, and the stakes too high for false confidence. What practitioners need is not a playbook that tells them exactly what to do, but a way of thinking that helps them work through decisions when the answers aren't clear: the ability to hold complexity without collapsing into either paralysis or recklessness; the discipline to measure what matters, even when measurement is hard; and the courage to make decisions under uncertainty while remaining accountable for the consequences.

AI companionship is not going away. The psychological mechanisms that drive it are too fundamental, the technological capabilities too advanced, and the human needs it addresses too real. The question was never whether people would form emotional bonds with AI systems. The question is what we, the researchers, designers, engineers, and organizations building these systems, will do with the responsibility that comes with being on the other side of those bonds.

That question doesn't have a final answer. It has a practice. And the practice begins with knowing what you don't know.

About the Author

Giada Pistilli is a philosopher and AI ethics researcher who has been studying the ethics of conversational AI since 2017, years before the technology became a mainstream concern. She holds a PhD in Philosophy from Sorbonne Université, where her doctoral research examined how moral philosophy can inform the design and governance of conversational agents. She remains an Associate Researcher at the Sorbonne Université—CNRS lab Sciences, Normes, Démocraties, and a Research Affiliate at the Machine Intelligence and Normative Theory (MINT) lab.

Her published research spans AI ethics, value alignment, multilingual model evaluation, and human–AI companionship, with work presented at NeurIPS, FAccT, AAAI/ACM AIES, NAACL, and ICLR. Her insights on these topics have been featured in *Nature*, *The New York Times*, and *The Washington Post*, among other international outlets.

She spent nearly four years as Principal Ethicist at Hugging Face, where she shaped ethical frameworks for one of the largest open-source AI platforms in the world and co-chaired the ethics working group of BigScience, the international research collaboration behind the multilingual language model BLOOM. She now works on model behavior and safety at a major European AI company, where she builds evaluation benchmarks for multilingual and culturally nuanced AI.

Her broader research examines how AI systems encode values, shape social relations, and interact with people across cultures and languages. This book draws on one thread of that work: what happens when those interactions become relationships.

Her perspective is uncommon in this space: trained in moral philosophy, embedded in engineering teams, and working across the full cycle from research to deployment. This book is the product of that position.

She lives in Paris with her husband, daughter, and cat.

Index

A

adaptation techniques, 122
adaptive systems
  behavioral monitoring, 150
  boundary adjustment, 148–149
  context-aware intervention, 149–150
  privacy, 150
adjustable boundary, 142
  comprehensibility challenge, 144–145
  user choice, structuring, 142–144
adversarial training, 126–127
advertising-supported model, 169
age verification, 140
  limits of, 173–174
AI as lover, 30–32
  designing endings, 161–162
  safety protocols, 111–112
AI companions
  availability, 11
  definition, 9
  emotional connection, 1–2
  ethical frameworks, 4
  evolution of, 12–14
  human–AI interaction, 1–2
  memory management, 3
  mental health support, 23
  technical challenges, 3
  workplace transformation, 23

AI dependency
preference for AI feedback, 28
vs. support, 75–76
AI identity, 186
AI-native communities, 25
AI relationship literacy, 45
AI systems
capabilities, 18
emergent social behaviors, 18
fake news generation, 17
annotators, 123–124, 129, 130
anomaly detection, 158
anthropomorphism, 21, 89–90, 102
artificial intimacy
anthropomorphism, 89–90
cognitive dissonance, 87–88
emotional reciprocity, 90
empathy, 90
memory construction, 88–89
theory of mind, 89–90
attachment-related harms, 174
attachment styles
anxious attachment, 84–85
avoidant attachment, 85
romantic attachments, 85
attachment theory, 83
attribution theory, 89
automated detection, 109, 157–158
autonomy
asymmetry of attachment, 141–142
harm principle, 139–140
paternalism, 140–141
vs. protection, 147

B

Bard (Google), 16
behavioral indicators, 148
boundaries
circumvention, 119–120
customization, 142–144
by design, 131
boundary-setting
empathetic, 100
monitoring systems, 114
paternalism *vs.* user agency, 110–111
safety protocols, 111–114
boundary-violating response, 125

C

Character.AI, 169, 173
chatbot-based CBT, 40
ChatGPT
conversational interface, 17

failure points, 106–107
harmful advice, 27–28
personal conversations, 17
romantic engagement, 30–32
Claude, 16
Claude Sonnet 4, 132
cloud infrastructure, 18
cognitive dissonance theory, 87–88, 96
community signal monitoring, 158
companionship manipulation, 99
consistency
and personality, 64–68
relationship formation, 159
constitutional AI, 125–126, 133
content regulation, limits of, 172–173
context-aware intervention, 149–150
context window
limitations, 120
reset, 30, 81
conversational AI, 4, 11, 15
core architectures
development environment, 58–60
ethical frameworks, 57–58
mechanical foundation, 55–56
model inference, 56
co-regulation, 84
cosine similarity, 71
crisis management, 105
ethical considerations, 109–110
expectations, 108–109
failure points, 106–107
limitations, 108–109
mental health infrastructure, 108
recognition and intervention, 94–95
resource integration challenges, 107–108
cultural differences, 25, 185

D

data quality issues, 130
dating platforms, 23
deadbots
cultural context, 36
deceased person simulation, 32–33
deceptions, 34
designing endings, 162–163
ethical concerns, 34–35
Grandpa Bot, 48
grief and mourning, 35
impersonation, 34–35
psychological effects, 36
safety protocols, 113–114
de-escalation pathways, 149

default-forgetting approach, 73
democratic governance, 26
dependency consolidation phase, 106
deployment
  designing endings, 160–163
  engagement metrics' issue, 155–157
  monitoring, 157–159
  testing, 154–155
  updates, 159–160
depression, 39, 91, 121
designing endings, 160–163
  communication transparency, 164
  cross-context principles, 164
  deadbots, 162–163
  disengagement risk, 161
  engagement calibration, 161
  romantic AI companions, 161–162
  therapeutic companions, 163
design responsibility, 49–51. *see also* responsible AI
design trade-offs
  availability *vs.* boundaries, 76–77
  individual *vs.* collective benefit, 77–78
  personalization *vs.* manipulation, 74–75
  support *vs.* dependency, 75–76
detection and response strategies, 100–101
developmental vulnerability, 93
development environment, 58–60
digital resurrection, 33, 36
digitized cemeteries, 34
direct preference optimization (DPO), 123–125, 133

E

elderly users vulnerabilities, 92
ELIZA
  effect, 13, 173
  emotional attachment, 12
  pattern recognition, 12
  transformation rules, 12
embedding-based approach, 68–71, 74
emotional analysis, 104
emotional exploitation
  crisis recognition, 94–95
  developmental vulnerability, 93
  identity formation, 93

individual psychology, 91
intervention thresholds, 94–95
life circumstances, 92
protection, 95–96
emotional reciprocity, 90
emotional recognition
cosine similarity, 71
embedding-based approach, 68–71
and manipulation, 74
response generation, 71
user inputs, 68, 71
and user vulnerability, 71–72
emotional regulation, 84, 90, 100, 104
empathy, 88, 90, 105
engagement
metrics, 155–157, 182
pressure, 145–146
escalation framework, 101, 105–106, 112
ethical considerations
crisis management, 109–110
emotional recognition and manipulation, 74
memory, 72–73
personality consistency *vs.* flexibility, 73
ethical frameworks, 4, 57–58
ethical memory dilemma, 64, 72–73
EU AI Act, 43–44, 122
evidence gaps, 184–186

F

fine-tuning, 122–123, 130
frameworks, limits of, 180–181

G

Gemma, 55
Gemma-3, 132
general-purpose AI assistants, 18, 19
technical design, 20
generational differences
AI relationships, 46
developmental paradox, 49
elderly users, 48
millennials, 48
technology adoption, 47
teen vulnerability, 47–48
generative AI, uses of, 2
Generative Pre-trained Transformer (GPT), 14–15
geographic isolation, 92
GPT-2, 15
GPT-3, 15–16
GPT-5-mini, 132
graduated response, 101
grief, 113–114

H

hard paternalism, 140–141
harm principle, 139–140
harness, 79
Hugging Face
  pipeline API, 56
  Transformers library, 55–56
human attachment systems, 83. *see also* psychology of attachment

I

identity formation, 93
implementation
  catastrophic forgetting, 130
  data quality issues, 130
  failure, 129–130
  initial setup phase, 127–128
  resource requirements, 128–129
  reward hacking, 129
  training instability, 129–130
industry standards, 175–176
institutional response
  complexity handling, 44
  cultural differences, 42
  education, 42–45
  emotional validation, 42–43
  governance structure, 42
  healthcare systems, 43, 45
  regulation, 43–44
  vulnerable populations, 45–46
  workplace policies, 45
Interactions and Machine Attachment (INTIMA), 128, 131–132, 154, 175
intervention hierarchy, 122–123
isolation reinforcement, 103

J

jailbreaking, 22, 97

K

knowledge-based systems, 13

L

LaMDA, 16
libertarian paternalism, 144–145
life circumstances, 92
LLaMA models, 13, 16
longitudinal effectiveness, 132–133

M

manipulation attempts, 99
  companionship manipulation, 99

detection and response strategies, 100–101
graduated responses, 101
mediated relationships, 10, 47
memory system
construction, 88–89
context windows, 61
conversation storage, 61
ethical considerations, 72–73
ethical issues, 64
retention strategies, 61–63
retrieval mechanisms, 61
mental health crises, 105
model inference, 56
multidimensional detection, 102–103

N

naming AI systems, 19–20
neurochemical addiction, 85–86

O

o4-mini, 131, 132
OpenAI
evolution, 132
Generative Pre-trained Transformer (GPT), 14–15
GPT-2, 15
GPT-3, 15–16

P

parasocial relationships, 86
paternalism, 140–141
pattern recognition, 18
personality, 64–67
consistency, 68, 78
consistency *vs.* flexibility, 73
Phi-4, 131–132
platform governance
cost, 147
cultural adaptation, 147
engagement as structural pressure, 145–146
individual benefit *vs.* collective impact, 147
user autonomy *vs.* user protection, 147
post-generation filtering, 122
post-training alignment, 123
adversarial training, 126–127
constitutional AI, 125–126
direct preference optimization (DPO), 124–125
red-teaming, 126–127
reinforcement learning from human feedback (RLHF), 123–124
pre-deployment testing, 154
prevention strategies, 100

privacy
  considerations, 109
  ELIZA, 13
  user, 114, 150
production monitoring, 157–159
prompt-based systems, 120
protection, users, 95–96
proximity imperative, 83–84
psychological vulnerabilities, 27–28, 91
psychology of attachment
  AI risk, 84–85
  emotional regulation, 84
  neurochemical addiction, 85–86
  parasocial relationships, 86
  proximity imperative, 83–84
  safe haven, 84
  styles, 84–85
purpose-built companion, 18–19

R

random sampling, 158
reciprocity gap, 141
red-teaming, 126–127, 155
reframing techniques, 119–120
regulation
  category issue, 172
  limits of age restrictions, 173–174
  limits of content regulation, 172–173
  limits of transparency, 173
  well-being requirements, 174
regulatory compliance, 122
reinforcement learning from human feedback (RLHF), 24, 123–124, 133
resolution strategies, 87
response inconsistency, 121
responsible AI
  engagement economy, 169–170
  expertise and power gap, 170–171
  inquiry culture, 187
  limits of organizational action, 168–169
  practice under uncertainty, 186–189
  scaling, 171
  user loss, 169
responsible development, 49–51
responsible iteration, 183
retention strategies, 63, 78, 103
reward hacking, 24, 124, 129
runtime interventions, limits of, 120–121

S

safety protocols
  AI as lover, 111–112
  AI as therapist, 112–113
  deadbots, 113–114
self-supervised learning, 14
SmarterChild, 13
social anxiety, 24, 91, 96
social contagion
  network effects, 44
  professional adoption, 44
  protection challenge, 46
social impact
  AI dependency, 28
  generational gaps, 46–49
  manifestations of AI companionship, 29–41
  psychological vulnerabilities, 27–28
social media pattern, 181
social robotics, 25
social stratification, 25
soft paternalism, 140–141
software updates, 159–160
statistical pattern-matching, 55, 56
subscription-based companion, 170
Super Brain, 33–34
sycophancy, 24, 102–103
system constraints, 176–177

T

technical safeguards, 97
teen vulnerability, 47–48
template-based responses, 71
temporal patterns, 148
testing, 154–155
theory of mind, 89–90
therapeutic AI companions
  access to care, 38
  chatbot-based CBT, 40
  clinical validation, 40
  dependency, 39–40
  designing endings, 163
  regulation, 40–41
  relationships, 39–40
  risks, 39, 41
  safety protocols, 112–113
  treatment gap, 38
  Woebot, 37–38
therapy industry, 23
three-pillar approach, 60–61
  emotional recognition, 68–72
  memory, 61–64
  personality, 64–67
tokenization, 55
training-level interventions, 128
trajectory analysis, 148

Transformer
architecture, 13, 14
attention mechanism, 15–16
library, 55–56
Transformer Reinforcement Learning (TRL), 128
transparency
limits of, 173
requirement, 141–142

U

uncanny valley effect, 34, 67
user
migration, 168–169
privacy, 150
vulnerability, 71–72
user attachment
bonds with AI, 81–82
psychology of, 83–86
user-centered design, 50
user interaction patterns
anthropomorphism, 21
emotional engagement, 19, 22
jailbreaking, 22
memory, 20
personas, 19–20
rationalization mechanism, 20

V

vulnerable populations
elders, 46
mental health conditions, 46
minors, 45–46
teenager, 121

W

well-being metrics, 170, 182
Woebot, 37–38
workplace transformation, 23

Y

young adults
challenges, 93
preference for AI, 23